The Hope of Glory

A Devotional Guide
For Older Adults

Volume One

Christ in you, the hope of glory.
COLOSSIANS 1:27

Nancy Parker Brummett

Lighthouse Publishing
of the Carolinas

www.lighthousepublishingofthecarolinas.com

Date	Lesson	Led by
2-28-17	#55 Love	Patricia + Roger
3-26-17	#38 old days	Patricia + Roger + Shirly Estr
4-23-17	#28 start from	Joan, Roger, Shirley
5-28-17	Joy (14)	Tom + Kathleen Masters
6-25-17	#40 Hear Gods way	Joe + Laurel Nichols
7-23-17	#17 God in Need	Joan Foster - Shirly Est. Ashley, Peter Kue + Grace Way
8-27-17	—	Tom + Kathleen Masters
10-22-17	#29	Jo + Laurel Nichols
11-26-17	#53 (gratitude)	Joan, Roger, Shirley
3-25-18	#41 Sunrise Hope	Joan, Roger, Shirley + Jim —
4-22-18	Earthday - Dr Seuss - The Lorax	
6-24-18	#33 why worry?	Joan, Roger, Shirley + Jim
9-23-18	#2 change	Joan, Shirley + Jim
10-28-18	— Tom + Kathy Masters — His own Sermon	
11-25-18	#3.	Joe + Laurel.
12-23-18	- Carol Sing - 2PM	
1-27-19	- Patricia, Carol & MacDonall Phil 4:4-8	
2-24-19	3-5th graders - Glenn Ferguson Play - Grace	
3-24-19	- Tom Masters —	
4-28-19	— 3-5th graders— GF- Play ✓	
5-26-19	- P Tuor, J Wright S+J Estes - Memorial + Freedom	
6-23-19	- #22 Practicing Patience - Joan F.	
7-__-19	Laurel + Joe - Laurels Testimony	
10-27-19	#48 Blessed Assurance - Nita North, MacDonalds, Joan F.	
11-24-19	- Elem. kids - Play - Glenn + Dave Megers	
12-22-19	- PT - Carol sing - Interruptions —	

Praise for *The Hope of Glory*

"GROWING OLD may not always be easy, but it can be a joyful journey if we choose to live out our faith in spite of our circumstances. Nancy Parker Brummett's *The Hope of Glory* is a great resource for older adults and those who love and care for them. With themes that are relevant to aging, each chapter's scripture, meditation, prayer and reflection questions will help older adults keep their eyes focused on God as they continue the journey through aging."

> —MISSY BUCHANAN, Speaker and Author of *My Story, My Song* with Robin Roberts and Lucimarian Roberts, *Living with Purpose in a Worn-Out Body*, and other books on aging and faith.

"NANCY HAS DONE AN OUTSTANDING JOB in compiling these precious lessons for older adults. They are excellent not only for a beginner, but also for seasoned teachers, as well as chaplains to use when ministering to residents in our communities' care centers. We at Crossroads Ministries will be utilizing this book for years to come."

> —KAY OWEN-LARSON, Founder and President Crossroads Ministries USA, Inc.

"*THE HOPE OF GLORY*—what a wonderful resource for sharing God's Word to our elderly! Nancy has blended Scripture, prayer, and meditations into an easy-to-use devotional that is inspiring and relevant to our seniors' time of life."

> —REX BISHOP Assisted Living Chaplain

THE HOPE OF GLORY BY NANCY PARKER BRUMMETT
Published by Lighthouse Publishing of the Carolinas
2333 Barton Oaks Dr., Raleigh, NC, 27614

ISBN 9781938499326
Copyright © 2014 by Nancy Parker Brummett
Cover photo illustration copyright © 2014 by Thomas Brummett
Author photo copyright © 2011 by Francesca McConnell
Interior design by Rhonda Dragomir of Dream Shapers

Available in print from your local bookstore, online, or from the publisher at:
www.lighthousepublishingofthecarolinas.com

For more information on this book and the author visit:
www.nancyparkerbrummett.com.

Brought to you by the creative team at LighthousePublishingoftheCarolinas.com.

Library of Congress Cataloging-in-Publication Data
Brummett, Nancy Parker.
The Hope of Glory/ Nancy Parker Brummett

Printed in the United States of America

Contents

Special Holiday Lessons

Dedicated to all the courageous, faithful older adults
I have been blessed to know.
—NPB

Introduction and Guidelines

The Hope of Glory is a devotional guide with 57 lessons for individuals over 65 and those leading weekly devotional hours for older adults in retirement homes, assisted living residences, nursing homes, senior centers, or Sunday school classes. The elderly in our society too often suffer from hopelessness, loneliness, and long days separated from the people they love and the communities in which they lived and worked. *The Hope of Glory* will give them eternal hope as it communicates the Gospel message and reminds them of who they are in God's eyes: not old and useless, but men and women created in His image who still have a life to live, a story to tell, and a future of eternal glory!

FOR INDIVIDUAL DEVOTIONS

If you are an older adult who would like to use *The Hope of Glory* for your daily devotions, simply work through the lessons at your own pace. Remember to turn to the back for lessons relevant to special holidays. It may help you remember your spiritual journey if you answer lesson questions in a personal journal.

FOR GROUP DEVOTIONS

To begin a class, visit a care facility near you and meet with the Executive Director and/or Activities Director. Allow them to review *The Hope of Glory* and receive their permission to go ahead. (Or meet with your pastor if you are offering the class in the church.) They will also help you advertise the class, determine the best time and place to meet, and gather attendees.

The Hope of Glory was field tested with groups of residents in assisted living facilities. Each lesson is designed to include group interaction and discussion and should take about one hour or less. Class length may vary depending on how long it takes to assemble, the number in the group, individual participation, and the number of hymns chosen.

GUIDELINES FOR GROUP FACILITATORS

Even if you have never led a Bible study or devotional hour before, *The Hope of Glory* will make it easy for you. Your willingness and heart to serve are the most important factors. Each lesson will guide you step-by-step as you read the lesson to the group. Make sure you speak loudly enough for everyone to hear. You may use the lessons in the order they appear in the book or skip around at will. (Select the five holiday lessons in the back as needed.)

You will notice that each numbered lesson has a title, or theme, a Key Verse (write this on a board in the meeting room if possible), and an Opening Prayer. The Introduction to each lesson elaborates on the theme for that class and stimulates the initial discussion period. Be willing to wait for responses to the questions. If you don't get responses to the questions as asked, try restating them in a slightly different way. As you become comfortable with the group, ask quieter individuals what they are thinking. If necessary, gently ask group members who dominate the discussions to allow others a turn to share.

The Scriptures and Quotes are also related to the theme for each lesson. (All Scripture verses are from the New International Version of the Bible, unless otherwise noted.) As you read these verses and quotes, pause after each one. If you are familiar with the verse, you might add some context from the Bible. Each entry can be a starting point for additional discussion and teaching if you choose, but this is optional and isn't necessary with each entry. Let the Holy Spirit lead the discussion! Some residents may want to bring their Bibles and look up verses as you go. Of course this is good, just allow for the extra time it will take.

The Meditation section of each lesson presents the theme's Biblical meaning and suggests a behavioral or attitude change as we all grow in Christ. It will frequently present the Gospel message as well, so be sensitive to group members who may want to pray privately after class to accept Jesus as their Savior for the first time. Nothing that happens is more important than that!

Each Meditation will be followed by a second series of questions for discussion, A Thought to Share, and a Suggestion for the Week. Then the real fun begins as you introduce one or more hymns for the group to sing together. It is wonderful if you have a pianist and hymnbooks for the class, but it is not necessary. Handing out copies of the words in lieu of hymnbooks increases participation. (Some attendees will want to take the words with them at the end of class.)

The hymns suggested are familiar to most, and even those who sit quietly through the discussion periods will often become animated and sing joyfully during the singing time. I will never forget the day a member of one of my classes suggested we sing "The Battle Hymn of the Republic" again—but that this time we march around the room. There we went, walkers, canes and all! Music is so important as it has the power to trigger the brain and restore memories. If you don't have accompaniment, don't hesitate to just start singing and "make a joyful noise!" You will be blessed by the class response.

After each class, ask each member in attendance for personal prayer requests or praises. This is often when you learn how each individual is really doing and what challenges he or she is facing. (Record requests to create a history of attendees and a record of what God is doing.) Close by offering these requests to the Lord—along with a lot of praise for the time you've had together. Information revealed by group members should be kept confidential unless you are concerned; then ask their permission to share with caregivers.

Announce the theme for the next lesson to motivate group members to return. The format of *The Hope of Glory* also makes it easy for new people to join the class at any time.

ADDITIONAL THOUGHTS

Older adults often aren't interested in doing the homework required in traditional Bible studies. Difficulties seeing or writing may make fill-in-the-blank studies too challenging. That's why *The Hope of Glory* is designed to give them a rich, Bible-based devotional time without the hassle of books or homework.

Attendees do seem to appreciate a treat each week, however! It doesn't have to be anything fancy, but a plate of cookies or banana bread served with coffee or water will enhance the experience for everyone. It also helps to have something tactile to pass around in the group. For instance, for the lesson on "How God Uses Change," you may want to bring in a branch with fall leaves or a flower in bloom. For the lesson on "Remembering Spiritual Milestones," consider passing around a basket of smooth, small stones for each group member to take one. Other "take-aways" are often appreciated, too, but remember that most residents of care facilities have limited space in their rooms.

Henri Nouwen wrote, "As long as we think that caring means only being nice and friendly to old people, paying them a visit, bringing them a flower, or offering them a ride, we are apt to forget how much more important it is for us to be willing and able to be present to those we care for…Only as we enter into solidarity with the aging and speak out of common experience can we help others to discover the freedom of old age."[1]

If you are comfortable with your own aging, confident in your faith, and have an attitude of humility and a sense of humor, you will find leading these sessions quite rewarding. And yet there will be days when you realize it was the interaction between group members that was the most important reason for coming together. Be yourself and be willing to share your own experiences and spiritual journey. Soon you will develop warm relationships with those in your group, and you will be blessed as much or more than they will. Laughter and hugs go a long way to smooth over anything that may go wrong! Dispense both generously. Let the Holy Spirit be your guide, and may you sense the Lord's pleasure as you willingly serve those He loves. God bless you.

—NPB

LESSON 1

All Things Work Together

KEY VERSE

And we know that in all things God works for the good of those who love him, who have been called according to his purpose.
ROMANS 8:28

OPENING PRAYER

LORD, SO OFTEN IT'S HARD for us to understand why things happen the way they do. But we derive such comfort from knowing that everything that happens is in Your will for us. Thank You, Lord, for promising that You will work all things together for our good so that we might come closer to Your ultimate goal for us, which is to make us more like Your Son. In His name we pray, amen.

INTRODUCTION

It's easy for us to believe that God is in control when things are going well. However, we can begin to wonder where God is when a spouse dies, a loved one is ill, or a friend is suffering through the loss of a job or the heartache of a broken relationship.

There is a story about a little boy who told his grandma "everything is going wrong." He got in trouble at school, his brother hit him, and he has a bad cold. Meanwhile, the grandma is baking a cake. She asks her grandson if he would like a snack, which of course he would.

"Here, have some cooking oil," the grandmother says.

"Yuck," says the boy.

"How about a couple of raw eggs?"

"Gross, Grandma!"

"Would you like some flour then? Or maybe baking soda?"

"Grandma, those things are all yucky!" the boy says.

The grandmother replies that all those things seem bad by themselves, but when they are put together in the right way, they make a wonderfully delicious cake! God works the same way. Many times we wonder why He would let us go through bad or difficult times. But He knows that, when He puts everything together at the end of our lives, the result will be that we are closer to Him. In this way, it will all work together for our good.

For Reflection or Discussion

- Was there a time in your life when you found it hard to see God's hand at work in the midst of your circumstances?
- As you look back on that situation, can you begin to see how God took something bad and made something good come of it?
- What's happening to you now that you find hard to understand in light of God's promise to work all things together for your ultimate good?

Scriptures and Quotes

You intended to harm me, but God intended it for good to accomplish what is now being done, the saving of many lives.
GENESIS 50:20

The Lord is righteous in all his ways and loving toward all he has made.
PSALM 145:17

"For I know the plans I have for you," declares the Lord, "plans to prosper you and not to harm you, plans to give you hope and a future."

JEREMIAH 29:11
*Jesus replied, "You do not realize now what I am doing,
but later you will understand."*
JOHN 13:7

We live by faith, not by sight.
2 CORINTHIANS 5:7

*In a thousand trials, it is not just five hundred of them that work "for the
good" of the believer, but nine hundred and ninety-nine, plus one.*[2]
GEORGE MUELLER

*I may not understand, Lord, but one day I shall see
Thy loving hand was taking pains to fashion me like Thee.*
AUTHOR UNKNOWN

MEDITATION

The Bible is full of stories of people who were in the midst
of difficult circumstances and might have questioned why God
was doing what He was doing. Joseph was sold into slavery by his
brothers. Abraham was asked to sacrifice his only son Isaac, a son God
had promised him and for whom he and his wife Sarah had prayed
for many years. In Hebrews, Chapter 11, we read about others who
died without seeing what God was doing through the circumstances
in their lives, but they died believing that He was in control. *Now
faith is being sure of what we hope for and certain of what we do not see,*
we read in Hebrews 11:1. That faith is based not on what we see and
know, but on what we believe to be true through the reading of God's
word.

The challenge believers have today is to remember that we can
trust God's heart even when we don't understand the work of His
hands. We can draw faith from the things we see working together
in this world because we know God has filled His creation with
knowledge about the mysteries of life.

A scrap of material may seem useless, but when combined with
other scraps of various shapes and sizes it becomes part of a beautiful
patchwork quilt. One note from a musical instrument may sound

dissonant or harsh, but when played at the right time in the company of other instruments, it becomes a beautiful symphony! So it is with the words we speak and the events of our lives—for as long as we live. God will work all these things together for our good.

FOR REFLECTION OR DISCUSSION

- God promises to answer our prayers. Have you ever wondered why He was allowing something in your life only to pray about it and receive His answer through prayer?
- Sometimes we draw faith for the present from events of the past. Can you remember a time when God revealed His plan to you and thus increased your faith for the situation in which you found yourself?
- How can we encourage others to be faithful and trust God's hand in their lives in the midst of hard times?

A THOUGHT TO SHARE

Our future is secure when we trust God with our present.

SUGGESTION FOR THE WEEK

Share the above thought or Romans 8:28 with others this week. Help them see how something that seemed like a trial turned into a blessing or brought them closer to God.

SUGGESTED HYMNS

- He's Got the Whole World in His Hands
- Faith of Our Fathers

PRAYER REQUESTS AND CLOSING PRAYER

Lesson 2
How God Uses Change

Key Verse

There is a time for everything, and a season for every activity under heaven.
Ecclesiastes 3:1

Opening Prayer

Lord, we confess to You that change scares us. We like for things to stay the same because we find comfort in the familiar, but we trust that all the changes we experience are directed by You. Keep us strong in the midst of them. In Jesus' name, amen.

Introduction

Try as we might, we can't stop changes from happening. We fondly remember the little boys and girls we cuddled on our laps, but now we see grown men or women standing before us with children, and maybe even grandchildren, of their own. Our favorite doctor retires and we have to find a new one. A rolling meadow in our town becomes an apartment complex, and the family home we remember is demolished to make way for a parking lot. Change is inevitable.

Changes in our living arrangements or our routine can especially rattle us. A favorite chair may not make the move, and other things we are used to having at hand may not be there anymore. Even when the new situation has many positive aspects, and may be in our best interest, we can still be shaken just by the change it represents.

We can't stop change, but we can control our response to it. In fact, psychologists tell us that adapting to change is one way to keep our minds active and our outlook bright. Some adaptations are relatively simple. When summer changes to fall, we put on a sweater, and when fall becomes winter, we trade the sweater for a heavy coat. Yet those changes are easy to accept compared to some of the major, life-shaking ones. These might include the loss of a spouse or a move from a home where we've lived for decades into a residential care facility. Our ability to adjust to such monumental changes is directly related to our ability to keep our eyes fixed on the unchanging quality of God's love for us.

For Reflection or Discussion

- We know that change is a part of God's plan for His creation when we see the change of seasons. What's your favorite season? Do you welcome the change from one season to the next?
- Why do you think many people find change so frightening? What changes in your life were the hardest for you to face?
- If you have traded living alone for living in a residential care facility, that was a major life change. How are you coping with it?

Scriptures and Quotes

Lord, you have been our dwelling place
throughout all generations.
Psalm 90:1

But from everlasting to everlasting the Lord's love
is with those who fear him, and his righteousness
with their children's children.
Psalm 103:17

He has made everything beautiful in its time.
Ecclesiastes 3:11

I the Lord do not change. So you, O descendants of Jacob,
are not destroyed.
Malachi 3:6

Jesus Christ is the same yesterday and today and forever.
HEBREWS 13:8

Every good and perfect gift is from above, coming down from the Father of the heavenly lights, who does not change like shifting shadows.
JAMES 1:17

God, grant me the serenity to accept the things I cannot change, the courage to change the things I can, and the wisdom to know the difference.[3]
REINHOLD NIEBUHR

MEDITATION

In Ecclesiastes, Chapter 3, the Bible gives us a long list of changes we can expect. There is, we read, a time to be born and a time to die, a time to plant and a time to uproot, a time to weep and a time to laugh, and many more. Each specific time that occurs involves change, yet we can never be completely prepared for all that change brings, can we?

By observing the world, we see that God uses change as a part of life. That doesn't take away the pain of the losses we suffer at the hands of change. The empty-nester mom cries in the grocery store when she hears a teenage boy call out "mom" and realizes the voice couldn't be her son's anymore. The father holds back tears as he walks his daughter down the church aisle to meet her groom. Even such positive changes bring us pain.

How then do we deal with the more monumental changes life brings: the loss of a family home, a child, or a spouse? Change changes *us*, there's no doubt about it. But it can change us in a way that brings us closer to God. That happens when we focus on His unchanging character and His unchanging love for us, not on what is changing around us.

God uses time to change us for the better. The longer we know God and learn about His precepts, the more like Him we become. Philippians 1:6 reads: *He who began a good work in you will carry it on to completion until the day of Christ Jesus.* This sanctification process continues throughout our lives as we grow closer to being like Jesus every day. That's a change we can celebrate!

For Reflection or Discussion

- Have you ever thought about the unchanging character of God? What comfort can you draw from His consistent presence in your life?
- What changes in your life resulted in your growing more beautiful in God's eyes? Which ones brought you closer to Him?
- Are you worried about changes that may happen in the future? How can focusing on God help you face those changes with faith and courage?

A Thought to Share

> *I know not what tomorrow holds,*
> *but I know who holds tomorrow.*

Suggestion for the Week

Tell at least one other person of a change in circumstance or attitude that you hope to make for the better this week.

Suggested Hymns

- A Mighty Fortress Is Our God
- Because He Lives

Prayer Requests and Closing Prayer

Lesson 3
Living in Community

Key Verse

How good and pleasant it is when brothers live together in unity!
Psalm 133:1

Opening Prayer

Lord, how blessed we are not to be in this world alone, but to have the fellowship of others around us. We know that, as You have promised, You are also a part of every gathering of those who believe in you. Thank You for your presence, Lord, and help us to see Your will for us as we live in community with others. In Jesus' name, amen.

Introduction

We are stronger, and even become clearer about who we are and how we fit into the world, when we are in the company of others. Together we can accomplish feats we cannot do alone. The Pilgrims traveled together in ships to a new world and created communities along the Atlantic coast. The pioneers traveled together in wagon trains and created towns in the West, with each person supplying a vital part of what they needed to make the new communities thrive.

Studies have shown that older people who live in community with others, have friends, and regular, positive contacts with family members, are far less likely to suffer from dementia or depression than those who live alone. So whether we are part of a neighborhood and church that provides a sense of community or we are living in a residential care facility with others, being a part of a community can be important to our physical, emotional and spiritual well-being.

Yet it can be difficult to live in close proximity with others, can't it? We all have personal preferences and desires that dictate how we want to live out our days. Sometimes we find it difficult to accept that others may think differently. Throughout our lives, we will connect more easily with some people than with others, but it is easier to get along when believers in Jesus Christ are together in one place. The common faith that binds us is strong, and more important than any personality differences. God, who claims us as His children, binds us together as family.

For Reflection or Discussion

- Think back to communities you have been a part of in the past. Was there a time in your life when you felt you truly belonged as a member of a certain neighborhood, work group or church group?
- What was your role in the setting you just remembered? Did you tend to be a leader or a valuable contributor? What did you do that helped you develop a sense of belonging?
- Living in close proximity to others can be a big adjustment when you are used to living alone or with a spouse. What do you think are (or would be) the biggest challenges to living in community in a residential care facility? What can you do to make those challenges easier?

Scriptures and Quotes

"For where two or three come together in my name, there am I with them."
Matthew 18:20

But in fact God has arranged the parts in the body, every one of them, just as he wanted them to be. If they were all one part, where would the body be? As it is, there are many parts, but one body.
1 Corinthians 12:18-20

Let the peace of Christ rule in your hearts, since as members of one body
you were called to peace. And be thankful. Let the word of Christ dwell in
you richly as you teach and admonish one another with all wisdom, and
as you sing psalms, hymns and spiritual songs with
gratitude in your hearts to God.
COLOSSIANS 3:15-16

He died for us so that, whether we are awake or asleep, we may live
together with him. Therefore encourage one another and build
each other up, just as in fact you are doing.
1 THESSALONIANS 5:10-11

But if we walk in the light, as he is in the light, we have
fellowship with one another, and the blood of Jesus, his Son,
purifies us from all sin.
1 JOHN 1:7

But in Christ, the things we do not know others do, and we may know
them and enter into the enjoyment of them through others.
Let me stress that this is not just a comfortable thought. It is a
vital factor in the life of God's people. We cannot get
along without one another.[4]
WATCHMAN NEE

Let our life be one of self-sacrifice, always studying the
welfare of others, finding our highest joy in blessing others…
Fellow Christians, let us praise God! We are called to love
as Jesus loves, as God loves.[5]
ANDREW MURRAY

MEDITATION

Perhaps no theologian has spoken so eloquently and
comprehensively on the subject of Christian fellowship than the
German pastor and theologian Dietrich Bonhoeffer. Like the apostle
Paul, Bonhoeffer did much of his writing about the life of believers
while he was in prison. He was outspoken in his denouncement of
Adolph Hitler and was sent to prison in April, 1943. On April 8,

1945, he was hanged at the concentration camp in Flossenbürg. Following is an excerpt from Bonhoeffer's book, *Life Together*, which was translated into English and published in the United States in 1954:

> "Christianity means community through Jesus Christ and in Jesus Christ. No Christian community is more or less than this. Whether it be a brief, single encounter or the daily fellowship of years, Christian community is only this. We belong to one another only through and in Jesus Christ.
>
> "What does this mean? It means, first, that a Christian needs others because of Jesus Christ. It means, second, that a Christian comes to others only through Jesus Christ. It means, third, that in Jesus Christ we have been chosen from eternity, accepted in time, and united for eternity."[6]

God assures us that we have a place and a role to play whether we are part of our chosen community or one not of our choosing due to circumstances. We can always choose to make our community a better place just by determining to play our part in creating an environment of Christian fellowship.

For Reflection or Discussion

- Why do Christians need other believers?
- Was there a time in your life when God used someone else to show you His will for your life?
- How can those living in community help one another be stronger in their faith?

A Thought to Share

We truly can live "all for one and one for all" when Christ unites us.

Suggestion for the Week

In his teachings, Bonhoeffer encouraged Christians to see others as Christ sees them. Mother Teresa also encouraged the sisters who worked for her to look for Christ in every face. As you are a part of your community this week, make an effort to look for Christ in everyone you encounter.

Suggested Hymns

- In Christ There is No East or West
- Blest Be the Tie that Binds

Prayer Requests and Closing Prayer

NOTES

A Cheerful Heart

KEY VERSE

*All the days of the oppressed are wretched, but the cheerful heart
has a continual feast.*
PROVERBS 15:15

OPENING PRAYER

LORD, IT'S DIFFICULT FOR US to be cheerful day in and day out, especially when circumstances may leave us feeling anything but. It's on those days, Lord, that we ask You to give us the strength to offer a smile to someone, to look on the brighter side of an issue, and merely to praise You with a cheerful heart. In Your name we pray, amen.

INTRODUCTION

Those who are cheerful promote a feeling of cheer in others. If you have a cheerful heart, it will probably show on your face. It's hard to promote a feeling of cheer with a frown or a grumble, but as trite as it seems, a smile really can turn someone else's frown upside down.

Here are some anonymous quotes about smiles to bring one to your face:

A smile is an inexpensive facelift.

A smile is the light in the window of your face that tells people you're at home.

It takes 17 muscles to smile and 43 to frown. So smile—it's easier!

Wrinkles are there to tell us where smiles have been.

If you see someone without a smile, give them one of yours.

No one likes the fake cheerfulness we encounter day to day—the "have a nice day" comment from the person who just ignored us for hours, or the insincere smile from a person who is seething inside. But we all respond positively to a genuine smile on the face of someone with a cheerful heart, and we all feel better when we are cheerful. In fact, studies have proven that those with a positive, sunny outlook on life are most likely to have long, satisfying lives.

Walking through life with a positive attitude makes it possible to weather many difficulties, and keeping a sense of humor in the face of adversity has saved many from succumbing to depression. Of course, those who receive their joy from the Lord have a genuine reason to be cheerful.

FOR REFLECTION OR DISCUSSION

- Do you think you are more or less cheerful than you were 10 years ago? Why the change? Does this mean you smile more, or less?
- How do you tell the difference between someone with a cheerful heart and someone who is just pretending to be cheerful? Is there any merit in smiling even when you don't feel like it?
- Do you think it's true that what exists in our hearts shows on our faces? Why or why not?

SCRIPTURES AND QUOTES

An anxious heart weighs a man down,
but a kind word cheers him up.
PROVERBS 12:25

A happy heart makes the face cheerful,
but heartache crushes the spirit.
PROVERBS 15:13

A cheerful look brings joy to the heart,
and good news gives health to the bones.
PROVERBS 15:30

A cheerful heart is good medicine,
but a crushed spirit dries up the bones.
PROVERBS 17:22

God loves a cheerful giver.
2 CORINTHIANS 9:7

Then for the first time I saw, as in a flash, that the religion
of Christ ought to be, and was meant to be, to its possessors,
not something to make them miserable, but something
to make them happy; and I began then and there to ask
the Lord to show me the secret of a happy Christian life.[7]
HANNAH WHITALL SMITH

Of cheerfulness, or a good temper—
the more it is spent, the more of it remains.
RALPH WALDO EMERSON

MEDITATION

Authentic cheerfulness may show on our faces when we smile, but it originates in our hearts. Once the heart knows the true joy that comes from a personal relationship with God, that joy pervades our entire body, all the way to our bones, as we read in Proverbs, and we can be cheerful on even the most challenging of days.

Several times in the gospels it is recorded that Jesus said to His disciples, "be of good cheer." He gave this instruction in times of peril, as in the raging storm described in Matthew 14:27 (KJV). It reads, *But straightway Jesus spake unto them saying, "Be of good cheer; it is I, be not afraid."* In John 16:33 (KJV), just before His death on the cross, Jesus encouraged the disciples by saying, *"In this world ye shall have tribulation: but be of good cheer; I have overcome the world."*

Other versions of the Bible translate Jesus' exhortation to be of good cheer differently. In the NIV, the Matthew verse about the storm reads "Take courage!" and the verse in John about tribulation reads "But take heart!" Though in this instance we may prefer the words of the KJV, "Be of good cheer," certainly nothing is lost in translation.

It is impossible for us to be cheerful unless we also have courage and take heart.

Authentic cheerfulness is an act of courage, especially when we find ourselves in situations that more naturally lend themselves to a grumbling spirit than to cheerfulness. But we don't lose heart, because we know that with Jesus on our side it is possible to be of good cheer whatever storm or trouble may come our way.

For Reflection or Discussion

- What does Jesus' instruction to "be of good cheer" mean to you today?
- Who do you see on a regular basis who seems genuinely cheerful? How does his or her cheerfulness affect you?
- Would others describe you as a person with a cheerful heart? Why or why not?

A Thought to Share

Cheering someone else up is the best way to cheer ourselves up!

Suggestion for the Week

Share the above thought or one of the Proverbs about cheerfulness with another person this week. Is there someone you would like to cheer up? Begin by giving them a genuine smile that emanates from the authentic cheerfulness in your heart.

Suggested Hymns

- Joyful, Joyful, We Adore Thee
- Leaning on the Everlasting Arms

Prayer Requests and Closing Prayer

LESSON 5
The Contented Life

KEY VERSE

*I have learned the secret of being content in any and
every situation, whether well fed or hungry,
whether living in plenty or in want.*
PHILIPPIANS 4:12

OPENING PRAYER

LORD, HOW EASY IT IS FOR US to focus on what we do not have
instead of on the many blessings we do enjoy. Teach us to be content
in whatever situation we find ourselves, trusting that You will fulfill
Your promise to meet all our needs. May we learn to embrace the
peace of mind and calmness of heart that come with being truly
content in our situations and circumstances. In Your name we pray,
amen.

INTRODUCTION

Contentment can be hard to come by, can't it? Our needs and
our wants get intermingled, difficult to sort from one another, and a
feeling of discontent can invade our hearts.

When the Apostle Paul wrote that he had learned the secret
to being content in any circumstance, he was truly saying a
lot. Throughout the course of his ministry he endured many
circumstances that most of us would find less than satisfactory, to say
the least. He lists his various trials in 2 Corinthians, Chapter 11. Here
is just a partial list: *Five times I received from the Jews the forty lashes*

minus one. Three times I was beaten with rods, once I was stoned, three times I was shipwrecked. Paul was also imprisoned during his ministry and it was in prison that he wrote many of the epistles that we have in the Bible today. Even after all these trials, he could still express his true contentment.

In contrast, even though most of our lives are without such physical peril, we live in a culture that almost encourages discontent. Advertisers strive to convince us that we need the latest, greatest product in order to be happy. Our society focuses on the beauty of youth, not the wisdom and treasure of old age. Achievement and perfect health become our goals, and when we are older, it's easy to focus on all we have lost rather than on all we have.

Yet our contentment is almost assured when we, like Paul, focus on the blessings the Lord has bestowed upon us and the benefits of being in a relationship with Him.

FOR REFLECTION OR DISCUSSION

- Part of being content is learning the difference between needs and wants. How have you been able to make that distinction in your own life?
- What is the source of contentment for you? Is it based on what you have done or had in the past, or are you able to live in the present contentedly?
- What change could you make in your mind and heart that would help you to be more content in your present circumstances?

SCRIPTURES AND QUOTES

*Praise the Lord, O my soul, and forget not all his benefits—
who forgives all your sins and heals all your diseases, who
redeems your life from the pit and crowns you with love
and compassion, who satisfies your desires with good things
so that your youth is renewed like the eagle's.*
PSALM 103:2-5

The fear of the Lord leads to life: Then one rests content,
untouched by trouble.
PROVERBS 19:23

And my God will meet all your needs according to
his glorious riches in Christ Jesus.
PHILIPPIANS 4:19

But godliness with contentment is great gain. For we
brought nothing into this world, and we can take
nothing out of it. But if we have food and clothing,
we will be content with that.
1 TIMOTHY 6:6-8

Be content with what you have.
HEBREWS 13:5

Contentment comes not to those whose means are great,
but to those whose needs are few.
ANONYMOUS

I considered that He was always with me, that He was
even within me... This practice produced in me so high
an esteem for God that faith alone was
enough to satisfy all my needs.
BROTHER LAWRENCE

MEDITATION

Greek philosophers often used the word contentment to indicate that a person should have an inner-sufficiency. But when Paul uses this word, it's with the knowledge that believers can be content in spite of their circumstances not because of their own sufficiency, but because of Christ's sufficiency.

True contentment comes from knowing, without a doubt, that we are safe in God's hands for all eternity. Once we give our lives to Jesus Christ, we are His forever. He says in John 10:28: *"I give them* eternal life, and they shall never perish; no one can snatch them out of my hand."

For the believer, then, true contentment comes from trusting that God truly will meet all our needs and has our future secure. We can live a life of contentment once we begin to focus on that blessing, and to be truly grateful for all we have through Christ.

While we're present on this earth, however, being content is simply being satisfied with what we have. We pay less attention to any perceived deficits once we are able to recognize the blessings in our lives and be grateful for them. Instead, we can approach each day grateful for our circumstance and open to the blessings another day holds. Contentment and gratitude go together in this way. It's almost impossible to have one without the other.

Once we truly believe that the Lord will provide for our needs, a peaceful contentment comes easier for most of us.

For Reflection or Discussion

- What lessons have you learned in your lifetime about how to be content in the midst of every circumstance? Do you have a testimony similar to Paul's?
- How easy is it for you to accept that we brought nothing into this world and we can take nothing out of it?
- It's difficult to be content when those around you are not. How can you share your contentment with others?

A Thought to Share

Contentment is not having what you want
but rather wanting what you have.

Suggestion for the Week

Share the above quote or Philippians 4:12 with someone this week. Help them see how focusing on what they have instead of what they have lost can bring contentment and happiness.

Suggested Hymns

- Great is Thy Faithfulness
- Count Your Blessings

Prayer Requests and Closing Prayer

NOTES

LESSON 6
Finishing Well

KEY VERSE

Now finish the work, so that your eager willingness to do it may be matched by your completion of it, according to your means. For if the willingness is there, the gift is acceptable according to what one has, not according to what he does not have.
2 CORINTHIANS 8:11-12

OPENING PRAYER

LORD, WHEREVER OUR LIFE JOURNEY has taken us thus far, we want to be able to say, like the Apostle Paul, that we are finishing well. Bring to mind those things we can still do that we have left undone, Lord. Give us the words and thoughts that help us tie up the loose ends in our lives and in our spirits, and by Your grace we will finish well. In Your name we pray, amen.

INTRODUCTION

We all remember the advice our parents gave us about doing a job right or not doing it at all. Whether it's baking a pie or launching a new corporation, any job worth doing is worth completing well. A life full of half-finished projects is rarely very satisfying to anyone.

College freshmen are often confused about which course of study to follow, where to spend their extra time, and what degree they want to achieve. Most of them sort these things out so that, on graduation day, their parents and grandparents can beam with pride at their success because they finished well.

As we reach the later stages of life, many of our daily jobs are completed. Whether we reared a family, held down a job, or both, with retirement those jobs are done. Yet through our attitudes and actions, we can still endeavor to finish well the course set before us now.

For some of us, finishing well on a daily basis means going to bed with no regrets about how we spent the day. We've communicated with those we want to thank, we've shared a smile or extended a hand of friendship, we've been gracious and patient with those around us, and so the day ends well. A string of such days becomes a life well lived—a life that finishes well, and honors God in the process. Of course the true definition of finishing well is to leave this earth secure in the knowledge that we are moving on to eternal life through Christ Jesus.

For Reflection or Discussion

- Is the concept of "finishing well" a new one to you or is it something you've thought about quite a bit?
- Can you recall a time in your life when it took a lot of perseverance for you to finish a job well, but you did?
- What does "finishing well" mean to you at your present age and circumstance? Has your definition changed over the years?

Scriptures and Quotes

"My food," said Jesus, "is to do the will of him
who sent me and to finish his work."
John 4:34

"For the very work that the Father has given me to finish,
and which I am doing, testifies that the Father has sent me."
John 5:36

When he had received the drink, Jesus said, "It is finished."
With that, he bowed his head and gave up his spirit.
John 19:30

However, I consider my life worth nothing to me, if only I
may finish the race and complete the task the Lord Jesus
has given me—the task of testifying to the gospel of God's grace.
ACTS 20:24

I have fought the good fight, I have finished the race, I have kept the faith.
Now there is in store for me the crown of righteousness, which the Lord,
the righteous judge, will award to me on that day—and not only to me,
but also to all who have longed for his appearing.
2 TIMOTHY 4:7-8

The great lesson is that while we should always do our best to bring glory
to God with excellence, what really matters in life is not so much what we
do. What matters most is what God chooses to do through us.
This is why on my desk is a wonderful plaque with one of Mother Teresa's
favorite expressions: Faithfulness, Not Success.[8]
CHUCK COLSON

I used to ask God to help me. Then I asked if I might help Him.
I ended up by asking Him to do His work through me.
HUDSON TAYLOR

MEDITATION

Finishing well in life has more to do with our spiritual condition than any physical achievements. Whatever obstacles are in our way, God urges us to keep the faith and one day to finish well and receive "the crown of righteousness."

A dearly loved older woman confided to a visitor during the last days of her life that she felt like she was leaving behind "a suitcase full of old tissues." Although she had lived a remarkable life, been a well-respected teacher, author, wife, mother and grandmother, something felt unfinished to her. Surely when she got to heaven she discovered that whatever she felt she had left undone didn't really matter at all, because she truly did finish well in the sense that she died with the blessed assurance that she was going to be with the Lord.

Finishing well has less to do with success by the world's standards and more to do with where we are in our relationship to God. It's more about purity of heart and a clear conscience than about a hefty investment portfolio or long list of awards and achievements. We are able to finish well when we have told the people we love that we love them, when we have generously given of our time and energy to others, and when we are at peace with our eternal destination through acceptance of our Lord and Savior, Jesus Christ.

Throughout the Bible we see examples of people who may not have met the goals they set for themselves, but who still finished well in God's eyes. Moses never entered the Promised Land, and although it was his heart's desire, King David never rebuilt the temple in Jerusalem. Yet both of them finished well from God's perspective. Faithfulness and obedience to God are His keys to finishing well. If we can truly be available for God to use us for His purposes, then we will know true success.

Like Jesus, who gave us the best example of finishing well, we can rest in the knowledge that, when our life on earth is over, we still have eternity to spend with God. While we want to finish our time here well, the most remarkable aspect of finishing well in God's kingdom is that once we do, we are really just beginning!

For Reflection or Discussion

- What did Jesus mean when He said from the cross, "It is finished"?
- The verse in 2 Corinthians talks about finishing your work *according to your means*. What does this mean to you at this stage of your life?
- If someone asked you how they might "finish well" in life, what would your advice to them be?

A Thought to Share

It's never too late to finish what we started. The Lord wants us to finish well in terms of the work He has given us to do on this earth, so if you feel you have left things unfinished, turn them over to Him to complete. He will do so, to His glory.

Suggestion for the Week

Think of something small or monumental that you have left unfinished in your life and do one thing this week to bring it closer to completion. Remember, it may be an attitude or a relationship requiring your attention rather than a task. Or it may be the all important "unfinished business" of coming into relationship with God through faith in His Son. If you need help in "finishing well," ask for it.

Suggested Hymns

- A Charge to Keep I Have
- My Faith Looks Up to Thee
- Take My Life and Let it Be

Prayer Requests and Closing Prayer

NOTES

LESSON 7
Who Are We, Really?

KEY VERSE

For in Christ Jesus you are all children of God through faith.
GALATIANS 3:26 (NRSV)

OPENING PRAYER

LORD, HELP US TO SEE OURSELVES as You see us. You know each of us by name, Lord, and as our Creator, You know us better than we know ourselves. Help us to see that our true identity is ever, always who we are in Your eyes. In Your precious name we pray, amen.

INTRODUCTION

Sociologists and others specializing in the study and categorization of human beings have devised lots of tests to help us understand who we are, what it is that makes us unique, different from everyone else in the world. The Myers-Briggs test is just one of many used by schools and universities. Those who are tested are labeled with a series of letters explaining their tendency to be introverted or extroverted, or whether they tend to act based on fact or intuition. Another personality profile determines whether we are more like golden retrievers, lions, otters, or beavers.

While results from assessments like these are sometimes helpful in allowing us to understand ourselves and others, do they really give us a firm identity we can hold on to for the entire course of our lives?

All of us play many roles during our lifetimes: daughter, son, mother, father, grandparent—perhaps teacher, executive, pastor—many, many different roles. Some of these roles seem to define who we are for a period of time. Once we lose one role and move to the next, we feel confused about our identity and feel lost for a while. A woman whose last child goes to college may have such a period as she thinks, "I knew who I was when I was rearing my children, but who am I now?" Those who lose a spouse go through a similar period of loss in addition to their grief as they come to terms with the realization that they are no longer a husband or a wife. Counselors call these periods in our life "identity crises" and they always get our attention because they can be not only unsettling, but painful.

Fortunately, knowing who we are in Christ can alleviate all our insecurity.

For Reflection or Discussion

- Have you ever had one of the personality assessments described above? If so, what did you learn about yourself?
- Was there a time in your life when you were most comfortable with your identity—when you really knew who you were and what your purpose was? Talk about that time.
- What is your identity at this stage of your life? Are you more or less confident in who you are now than you were at a younger age? Why?

Scriptures and Quotes

Yet to all who received him, to those who believed in his name,
he gave the right to become children of God—children born
not of natural descent, nor of human decision
or a husband's will, but born of God.
John 1:12-13

The Spirit himself testifies with our spirit that we are God's children.
Now if we are children, then we are heirs—heirs of God
and co-heirs with Christ, if indeed we share in his sufferings
in order that we may also share in his glory.
Romans 8:16-17

Therefore, if anyone is in Christ, he is a new creation;
the old has gone, the new has come!
2 CORINTHIANS 5:17

We are therefore Christ's ambassadors, as though God
were making his appeal through us.
2 CORINTHIANS 5:20

How great is the love the Father has lavished on us, that we
should be called children of God!
1 JOHN 3:1

We must be willing to be either generals or gatekeepers, allotted
to our parts just as God wills and not as we choose.[9]
WATCHMAN NEE

God does not expect us to imitate Jesus Christ: He expects us
to allow the life of Jesus to be manifested in our mortal flesh.[10]
OSWALD CHAMBERS

MEDITATION

What comfort there is in knowing that, regardless of our personality type or the roles we play in life, our true identity is as a child of God once we believe in Him and trust in His promises.

Those who find their true identity in Christ are not easily shaken by the changes and trying circumstances life can offer. They may be perplexed from time to time, of course, but ultimately they know that they belong to God and are on the path that leads to eternal life with Him. When all is said and done, that is all that really matters.

We can rest assured that God forgives all our sins because of our faith in Jesus. We have been reconciled to God, and we are new creations in Christ and joint heirs with Him for all eternity! Those are glorious promises that bear much more importance and truth than any number of personality assessments we might encounter. Once someone has the blessed assurance that comes with understanding who they are in Christ, they have His power as well—the power to persevere through trials and illnesses, the power to break away from harmful behaviors or addictions, and the power to live each day for His glory because they are totally accepted and loved by Him.

The wonderful truths in the Bible about who we are in Christ should leave us with little doubt about our identity. God knows who we really are and why we are here. It's our job to embrace the identity He has given to us.

For Reflection or Discussion

- Have you ever thought of yourself as an ambassador for God? How does accepting this role influence your interactions with others?
- We often fret about what we will leave to our heirs. What are we inheriting from our heavenly Father? How can we pass it on to those who follow us?
- By faith, we are full heirs with Christ of all the glories of heaven and earth! How does this "inheritance" influence how you feel about yourself? What does it mean to you to be a child of God?

A Thought to Share

We will never have an identity crisis once we identify with Christ.

Suggestion for the Week

Spend some time in conversation with others you encounter this week to discover how your personalities are alike and different. Learn to appreciate at least one person whose personality differs greatly from your own. If you feel so led, be God's ambassador and share how our true identity is in Christ.

Suggested Hymns

- I Surrender All
- Just As I Am

Prayer Requests and Closing Prayer

LESSON 8

The Power of Prayer

KEY VERSE

Do not be anxious about anything, but in everything, by prayer and petition, with thanksgiving, present your requests to God.
PHILIPPIANS 4:6

OPENING PRAYER

LORD, HOW BLESSED WE ARE that we can come to You with our concerns any time, night or day, and You are never too busy to hear us. Thank you, Lord, for the gift of prayer. Teach us to tap into the power it provides for us to communicate with You and to know Your will for our lives. In Your name we pray, amen.

INTRODUCTION

Have you ever been in a situation where someone asks you to pray for someone, or for a difficult situation, just because they know you are a person of faith? Surely, anyone who walks with the Lord is happy to pray any time. But it is sad that these people don't understand that they, too, can approach the throne of God through prayer once they believe in Him. We serve a God who allows equal access to Him at all times.

Even people who don't have a life of faith at all will rarely turn down an offer of prayer, for even nonbelievers know there is power in prayer. It's impossible to live on this earth without hearing stories of lives changed, cures manifested, and dire situations reversed, all because someone prayed. God's answer to our prayers may be yes, no, or not now—but He always answers and no prayer is too trivial for Him!

Some people don't pray because they feel like they don't know how. They mistakenly believe that there is a wrong and a right way to pray, and that getting it wrong could be worse than not praying at all! Not so. Prayer is simply having a conversation with God, just as you would with any close friend. A formal prayer said in church is no more powerful than a whispered prayer in the waiting room of a doctor's office. God hears every prayer, and they are all sweet music to His ears. If we think He isn't answering our prayers, maybe we just aren't listening!

For Reflection or Discussion

- Why do you think some people are reluctant to pray?
- Is prayer a part of your daily life? Why or why not?
- Can you share a time in your life when you are sure you heard an answer to prayer?

Scriptures and Quotes

"But when you pray, go into your room, close the door, and pray to your Father, who is unseen."
MATTHEW 6:6

"And I will do whatever you ask in my name, so that the Son may bring glory to the Father."
JOHN 14:13

"Father, I want those you have given me to be with me where I am, and to see my glory, the glory you have given me because you loved me before the creation of the world."
JOHN 17:24

We do not know what we ought to pray for, but the Spirit himself intercedes for us with groans that words cannot express.
ROMANS 8:26

*Therefore confess your sins to each other and pray for
each other so that you may be healed. The prayer
of a righteous man is powerful and effective.*
JAMES 5:16

*This is the confidence we have in approaching God:
that if we ask anything according to his will, he hears us.*
1 JOHN 5:14

*Any concern too small to be turned into a prayer
is too small to be made into a burden.*[11]
CORRIE TEN BOOM

*Prayer changes things—either the situation
or the one who is praying.*
ANONYMOUS

MEDITATION

Prayers don't have to follow a certain format, and there is no wrong way to pray. However, the Bible does tell us there are some things that can block our prayers and keep them from being as effective as they could be. One of those things is unconfessed sin in our lives. When we know we are harboring ill feelings toward someone, or even have allowed the sins of doubt and despair to creep into our hearts and minds, we need to confess those sins before we pray. In fact, it's good to begin our prayer time with the Lord by asking His forgiveness for all our sins—those we acknowledge and those that may have conveniently escaped our attention!

Secondly, we should be sure there is no unforgiveness in our hearts toward others. Forgiveness not only frees us of the burden we carry when we don't forgive, but frees up our prayers, too! And every prayer we offer up should also praise the God who is always willing to listen—and be full of the gratitude we want to express to Him. Does this seem like a lot to remember? God hears even a "whisper prayer" or a "thought prayer," but for intentional prayer times with the Lord, the acronym ACTS can be helpful. We begin our prayer with ADORATION followed by CONFESSION, then we offer up

THANKSGIVING to the Lord, followed by any SUPPLICATION, or requests we want to make.

Jesus is our best example of how to pray. Throughout the Biblical accounts of His ministry, we read that He took time to get up early or retreat into the mountains to pray. He was in the Garden of Gethsemane praying for us the night before He died on the cross for our sins.

When we pray, where we pray, and how we pray isn't nearly as important as that we pray. As we grow older, it can be difficult to do many of the things we used to do to serve the Lord and others, but we can all pray. A good habit to get into is to make morning and evening prayers the "bookends" on your day. Simply open up your heart and have a conversation with God. Don't feel like you can only pray about the "big things" in life—nothing is too insignificant in His eyes.

FOR REFLECTION OR DISCUSSION

- Do you have the time or the inclination to be a "prayer warrior" for the Lord? It's a job with the power to affect change on earth as your prayers reverberate in heaven, and no one is too old to apply!
- Jesus taught us that we shouldn't babble endlessly when we pray, then He gave us an example of an effective prayer in Matthew 6:9-13. We know it as "The Lord's Prayer." (Recite together.) What other prayers do you know by heart? Perhaps a grace? Please share.
- We discussed the acronym ACTS as an effective prayer guideline. Are there others you know that you could share to help someone develop a richer prayer life? (Remember, there's no right or wrong way to pray.)

A THOUGHT TO SHARE

Prayer is when burdens change shoulders.

Suggestion for the Week

If prayer is a regular part of your day, spend some extra time in prayer this week. If you don't usually spend time in prayer, give it a try. You'll be so glad you did. If you don't know what to pray, open your Bible and pray the Scriptures. Prayer is the world's greatest wireless connection.

Suggested Hymns

- Sweet Hour of Prayer
- In the Garden

Prayer Requests and Closing Prayer

NOTES

LESSON 9

Knowing God

KEY VERSE

"Now this is eternal life: that they may know you, the only true God, and Jesus Christ whom you have sent."
JOHN 17:3

OPENING PRAYER

LORD, HOW BLESSED WE ARE that You want to really know us. Give us a hunger to know You, too. Not to just know about You, but to truly know You and have an intimate relationship with You. Thank You for making Yourself available to us any time, and any place we are. We want to know You, Lord. In Your name we pray, amen.

INTRODUCTION

An often-aired television commercial for a wireless phone service shows the cell phone user walking from point to point and saying, "Can you hear me now?" Isn't it possible that God is that persistent in trying to get through to us? His persistence is a blessing to us, for sure, but just why is it that we are so hard to reach?

The truth is God wants to connect with us because He knows us, and He wants us to know Him. In fact, establishing a relationship with us was so important to Him that He went far out of His way to come to earth and spend time with us. Isn't that how we get to know anyone, by spending time with them?

We develop an intimate relationship with others once we get to know them well. A relationship that is close, familiar and comfortable. We know all the big, important things about them—where they live, where they work, whether they are married—but we learn and cherish the little things we know about them, too. When we share intimate details with one another, friendships become relationships, and we truly know one another. Over time, we learn to trust one another, and a deep and loving connection is the result.

This is the kind of intimacy God wants to have with us. He wants us to know Him and to be in a love relationship with Him. Once we have that level of intimacy, we will also trust Him, confide in Him, and be connected to Him for all eternity.

For Reflection or Discussion

- Think of someone you know, or knew, really well. How did you get to know that person at such an intimate level?
- Did that person also know you really well? How do you know?
- What is the difference between knowing *about* God and knowing God?

Scriptures and Quotes

Love the Lord your God with all your heart and with all your soul and with all your strength.
DEUTERONOMY 6:5

The Lord is my shepherd; I shall not be in want.
He makes me lie down in green pastures,
he leads me beside quiet waters, he restores my soul.
PSALM 23:1-3

Whom have I in heaven but you?
And earth has nothing I desire besides you.
PSALM 73:25

Jesus answered: "Don't you know me, Philip?
Even after I have been among you such a long time?"
JOHN 14:9

"I no longer call you servants, for a servant does not know his master's business. Instead, I have called you friends, for everything that I learned from my Father I have made known to you."
JOHN 15:15

Faith is unutterable trust in God, trust which never dreams that He will not stand by us. [12]
OSWALD CHAMBERS

What is the one thing God wants from you? He wants you to love Him with all your being. Your experiencing God depends on your having this relationship of love. A love relationship with God is more important than any other single factor in your life. [13]
HENRY T. BLACKABY

MEDITATION

Theologian J. I. Packer wrote a book that has become a classic in Christian literature, *Knowing God.* He opens the chapter on "Knowing and Being Known" by stating, "What were we made for? To know God. What aim should we set ourselves in life? To know God. What is the 'eternal life' that Jesus gives? Knowledge of God…What is the best thing in life, bringing more joy, delight, and contentment than anything else? Knowledge of God."[14] Later in that same chapter he writes:

"What matters supremely, therefore, is not, in the last analysis, the fact that I know God, but the larger fact that underlies it—the fact that *He knows me.* I am graven on the palms of His hands. I am never out of His mind. All my knowledge of Him depends on His sustained initiative in knowing me. I know Him, because He first knew me, and continues to know me. He knows me as a friend, one who loves me; and there is no moment when His eye is off me, or His attention distracted from me, and no moment, therefore, when His care falters."[15]

So if that's what it looks like for God to know us, what does it look like when we know God? Packer says in the first chapter of his book that those who know God have great energy for God, have great thoughts of God, show great boldness for God, and have great contentment in God. Do any or all of those things describe us? If so, then perhaps we know God.

Many other authors have written about the joys of knowing God as well, but reading and studying isn't nearly as important as experiencing. Knowing God means you have an ongoing conversation with Him through prayer and you hear His voice speaking to you deep in your spirit. Knowing God means you trust Him all the time—whether you are presently hearing from Him or not. Knowing God means you are never alone. He knows us. The sooner we get to know Him, too, the more blessed we will be, in this life and the next. Hear Him when He speaks to you, and let your spirit respond, "I can hear You now!"

For Reflection or Discussion

- When we know people well, and have an intimate relationship with them, we trust them. What are you trusting God with today?
- Can you trust that you are always on God's mind, even when it seems He is silent? Why or why not?
- What one thing could you do this week in order to know God better and build a closer relationship with Him?

A Thought to Share

Our need for a relationship with God is a God-given need, so only God can satisfy it.

Suggestion for the Week

Spend some time listening to Christian radio, reading the Bible or another book about God and learn something about His character that you never knew before. Share what you learn with others.

Suggested Hymns

- What a Friend We Have in Jesus
- Nearer My God to Thee
- Be Thou My Vision

Prayer Requests and Closing Prayer

NOTES

LESSON 10
Being a Disciple

KEY VERSE

This is to my Father's glory, that you bear much fruit,
showing yourselves to be my disciples.
JOHN 15:8

OPENING PRAYER

LORD, HOW PRIVILEGED WE ARE to be called Your disciples once we believe in You and ask You to live out Your life through us. Be with us today as we consider what it means to be Your disciple, Lord. Give us Your insight and direction so that we may follow You with clear minds and devoted hearts. In Your name we pray, amen.

INTRODUCTION

The American Heritage College Dictionary defines a disciple as 1) one who assists in spreading the teaching of another or 2) an active adherent, as of a movement. In that regard, all of us are disciples of someone or something. For example, those who follow the teaching of psychologist Carl Jung are known as Jungians. Buddhists follow the teachings of Buddha and Muslims the teaching of Mohammed. Those who adhere to the movement to protect and save the earth are known as environmentalists—and those who prefer not to eat meat are vegetarians. Even those who would deny any allegiance to any particular teacher or movement may still be disciples, they just choose to follow their own desires and so are disciples of self.

To followers of Jesus Christ, known as Christians, the word disciple always brings to mind the twelve men closest to our Savior when He was walking among us. Jesus knew that His time on earth was limited, so He chose carefully those men who would be His closest associates. He knew it would be left to them to spread the Good News He came to earth to convey. Yet He didn't select the most powerful men of that age. Rather He primarily chose simple men of good character, including several fishermen. They weren't the wealthiest, the wisest, or the oldest of the population in Israel, but they were available and they were willing to follow Jesus.

After His crucifixion, the disciples scattered to preach the gospel message throughout the known world. In so doing, they created more disciples, and Christianity grew to be one of the most impactful faiths in the world.

For Reflection or Discussion

- What different movements have you followed in your lifetime? Think about allegiance to athletic teams and universities as well as philosophies, diets, or exercise programs.
- Other than Jesus Christ, who has inspired you in your lifetime to the point where you would say you were willing to spread their teaching to others?
- Did you ever think of yourself as a disciple of these movements or people? Why or why not?

Scriptures and Quotes

"And anyone who does not carry his cross and follow me cannot be my disciple."
LUKE 14:27

The next day Jesus decided to leave for Galilee. Finding Philip, he said to him, "Follow me."
JOHN 1:43

*To the Jews who had believed him, Jesus said, "If you hold
to my teaching, you are really my disciples. Then you will
know the truth, and the truth will set you free."*
JOHN 8:31-32

*"By this all men will know that you are my disciples,
if you love one another."*
JOHN 13:35

*We have put our hope in the living God, who is the Savior
of all men, and especially of those who believe.*
1 TIMOTHY 4:10

*A disciple of Christ is one who 1)believes His doctrine
2)rests on His sacrifice 3)imbibes [absorbs, takes in] His spirit and
4)imitates His example.* [16]
TODAY'S DICTIONARY OF THE BIBLE

If it is hard to follow Jesus, and it is, it is harder not to follow Him.[17]
WALTER A. HENRICHSEN

MEDITATION

So what does it mean to be a disciple of Jesus Christ? In Luke
9:23, Jesus said, *"If anyone would come after me, he must deny himself
and take up his cross daily and follow me."* The Living Bible translation
reads: *"Anyone who wants to follow me must put aside his own desires
and conveniences and carry his cross with him every day and keep close to
me!"*

However it is translated, this is a strong statement from Christ
to His followers. To pick up our cross daily means to deny our own
selfish desires and wants and put our dedication to Christ first in our
lives. It means willful obedience to all of His teachings. It means we
aren't Christians, or followers of Christ, only on Sunday mornings,
but every day.

Most of us will not achieve such perfect discipleship this side
of heaven. Try as we might, we still have those days when our self
interests take precedence. But because our God is also a God of

compassion, Jesus understands our shortcomings and forgives us our human nature—all the while encouraging us to give it one more try tomorrow!

To be a disciple of someone means you are a student not only of his teachings, but of the teacher himself. The more time we spend with Jesus, the more intimately we will know Him, and the easier it will become for us to live as His disciples.

In his classic devotional *My Utmost for His Highest*, Oswald Chambers wrote: "Have I a personal history with Jesus Christ? The one sign of discipleship is intimate connection with Him, a knowledge of Jesus Christ which nothing can shake."[18] And once we have this knowledge, and the good news of salvation through faith in Christ, how can we keep from sharing it? In Matthew 28:19-20, Jesus left His followers with these words: *"Therefore go and make disciples of all nations, baptizing them in the name of the Father and of the Son and of the Holy Spirit, and teaching them to obey everything I have commanded you. And surely I am with you always, to the very end of the age."* With hearts full of gratitude, those of us who would be disciples of Jesus not only follow Him, but we also take up His command to go and eagerly share the truth we know with love and grace.

For Reflection or Discussion

- How difficult is it for you to pick up your cross daily? What does this mean to you at this point in your life?
- Do you think we are more effective as disciples of Christ by what we say, or by what we do? Why do you think this is true?
- How can you "be Christ" to someone else?

A Thought to Share

> *We are all following someone. Make sure your allegiance is not misplaced. Follow Jesus!*

Suggestion for the Week

A popular 20th century hymn says, "And they'll know we are Christians by our love, by our love, Yes, they'll know we are Christians by our love." This week, be a disciple of Christ by doing something loving for another person. If you do, you will feel His pleasure!

Suggested Hymns

- O Master, Let Me Walk with Thee
- They'll Know We Are Christians by Our Love
- Take My Life and Let It Be

Prayer Requests and Closing Prayer

NOTES

LESSON 11

Running the Race

KEY VERSE

I have fought the good fight, I have finished the race, I have kept the faith.
Now there is in store for me the crown of righteousness, which the Lord,
the righteous Judge, will award to me on that day—and not only to me,
but also to all who have longed for his appearing.
2 TIMOTHY 4:7-8

OPENING PRAYER

LORD, SOMETIMES IT SEEMS like we've been running the race for
such a very long time. Come alongside us, Lord. Run beside us that
we might finish strong and bring You the glory. Thank You, Lord,
for Your promises of our rewards to come. Keep us moving forward,
Lord, as we finish the race laid out before us. In Your name we pray,
amen.

INTRODUCTION

In ancient Rome a laurel wreath was often placed on the head of
the victor in athletic games. It was the most coveted prize of that time.
Also in Greece, where the Olympic Games originated, a wreath was a
common sign of victory. Paul, in writing to Timothy, talks about the
crown of righteousness being the prize at the end of this race we know
as life on earth. (We know that we become "righteous" not based on
anything we do, but because of our faith in Jesus Christ.)

A woman in her mid sixties decided to enter a race at a summer
sports event. She trained for weeks leading up to the event and signed
up to run in the 50-meter dash and the 100-meter dash. She had

never competed before, and so she arrived at the competition not sure if she would even be able to finish the races she had signed up to run. Not only did she finish, she won a medal in each! In one event, she was the only contestant in her age group, but that didn't matter. She had challenged herself and she had won—in more ways than one. Now she enjoys showing people a photo of herself with her two medals around her neck.

Paul was nearing the end of his life when he wrote the letters to Timothy. He compares his 30 years of ministry to an athlete running a race. In much the same way, each of us is running our own race. However, this race isn't about winning. It's about doing our personal best and keeping the faith until we reach the finish line!

FOR REFLECTION OR DISCUSSION

- Were you athletic as a young person? In what sports did you participate?
- Can you relate to Paul's analogy of life being like a race? Why or why not?
- What is the prize you hope to receive at the end of your race?

SCRIPTURES AND QUOTES

However, I consider my life worth nothing to me, if only I may finish the race and complete the task the Lord Jesus has given me— the task of testifying to the gospel of God's grace.
ACTS 20:24

He will keep you strong to the end, so that you will be blameless on the day of our Lord Jesus Christ.
1 CORINTHIANS 1:8

Everyone who competes in the games goes into strict training. They do it to get a crown that will not last; but we do it to get a crown that will last forever.
1 CORINTHIANS 9:25

You were running a good race. Who cut in on you
and kept you from obeying the truth?
GALATIANS 5:7

But one thing I do: Forgetting what is behind and straining toward
what is ahead, I press on toward the goal to win the prize for which
God has called me heavenward in Christ Jesus.
PHILIPPIANS 3:13-14

Therefore, since we are surrounded by such a great cloud of witnesses,
let us throw off everything that hinders and the sin that so easily entangles,
and let us run with perseverance the race marked out for us.
HEBREWS 12:1

Therefore may we be content to share in the battle, for we will soon
wear a crown of reward and wave a palm branch of praise.[19]
CHARLES H. SPURGEON

MEDITATION

Biblical scholars suggest several meanings for the crown of righteousness of which Paul speaks. They say he could be referring to a crown given as a reward for a righteous life, a crown consisting of righteousness, or a crown given righteously (justly) by God, the righteous judge. Of course, none of us is righteous through his or her own strength or actions, but only through Jesus' death on the cross and our acceptance of salvation through Him. The crown we receive will be rewarded on that day—the day of Jesus' second coming.

None of us knows how much of our race is still ahead of us. We can look back over our lives and see lots of uphill runs and downhill coasts. We can see lots of twists and turns, and certainly can remember times we had to overcome obstacles or tripped and fell as we continued on our course. Yet still we keep running the race set before us.

Where do we get the perseverance to keep going? How is it we are able to keep getting up even when we fall down? The answer for many is the faith they have in Jesus Christ, and the strength they feel Him providing for each day that comes. We need to ask the Lord to keep us strong and faithful until we draw our last breath. Most of all, we need to ask Him to keep us from wasting precious time between now and then. For we want to keep running with the Lord right up to the finish line. If you haven't trusted in the Lord, now is the time to do so. Then you will be able to finish the race and claim the prize of eternal life with Him. That's the hope of glory that keeps us in the race!

For Reflection or Discussion

- As you look back over your life, can you see a time when someone or something "cut you off" and kept you from running the race the Lord gave you to run?
- What did it take for you to get back on course?
- What's the most difficult challenge you face in running your race from now to the finish line?

A Thought to Share

Most races are won by simply putting one foot in front of the other.

Suggestion for the Week

Think of something you could you do this week to help you stay fit for the race. It may be spiritual training that will help rather than physical training.

Suggested Hymns

- God of Grace and God of Glory
- It Is Well with My Soul
- Victory in Jesus

Prayer Requests and Closing Prayer

Lesson 12
Random Acts of Kindness

Key Verse

Be kind to one another, tenderhearted, forgiving one another,
as God in Christ has forgiven you.
Ephesians 4:32 (NRSV)

Opening Prayer

Lord, why is it that we see the faults of others so clearly but ignore our own until they accumulate to the point that we finally trip over them? We want to be more gracious than we are, Lord—to show the kindness and forgiveness to others that You have so generously bestowed on us. Give us Your compassionate heart, Lord. In Your name we pray, amen.

Introduction

We all know how much it means when others are kind to us, but do we make an effort to be kind to others? Do we make sure to insert at least one random act of kindness into each day we live? It can be something as simple as saying, "Thanks for doing your job so well," or "You have a great smile," but it becomes an encouragement to the recipient and so is an act of kindness.

One day a woman was in her neighborhood dry cleaners when she saw the young woman who usually waited on her in the back room in tears. She couldn't help but overhear that she was having problems at work. Two days later, before she went to pick up the cleaning, she stopped in the grocery store next door to pick up a few items. As she passed a display of floral bouquets, she felt the Holy

Spirit nudging her. "Why don't you pick up a bunch of those flowers and take them over to Amy at the dry cleaners?" He said.

"What pretty flowers!" Amy said when the woman walked in. "I'm glad you like them," she replied, "because they're for you! I couldn't help but notice you were having a bad day when I was here before."

The vase on the woman's kitchen table was empty that night, but the smile on Amy's face every time the generous woman came into the cleaners told her the Holy Spirit used a simple gesture to open the door to a more meaningful relationship between them. In God's economy, no act of kindness, however small, is ever wasted.

For Reflection or Discussion

- What's the last act of kindness you can remember someone doing for you?
- What's the last act of kindness you did for someone else?
- Do you think such acts happen spontaneously or need some forethought and planning?

Scriptures and Quotes

A kindhearted woman gains respect, but ruthless men gain only wealth. A kind man benefits himself, but a cruel man brings trouble on himself.
Proverbs 11:16-17

"Let your light shine before men, that they can see your good deeds and praise your Father in heaven."
Matthew 5:16

"So in everything, do to others what you would have them do to you."
Matthew 7:12

"But a Samaritan, as he traveled, came where the man was; and when he saw him, he took pity on him."
Luke 10:33

Make sure that nobody pays back wrong for wrong, but always
try to be kind to each other and to everyone else.
1 THESSALONIANS 5:15

Kind words can be short and easy to speak,
but their echoes are truly endless.[20]
MOTHER TERESA

The best portion of a good man's life,
His little, nameless, unremembered acts
Of kindness and love.
WILLIAM WORDSWORTH

MEDITATION

It may not be in our nature to be kind to others. Often life has
dealt us blows that leave us more bitter than kind. But once we have
the Holy Spirit dwelling inside us, all the fruit of the Spirit (Galatians
5:22-23), including kindness, will be evident in us. We aren't kind
because it is in our nature to be so. We are kind because kindness is
an integral part of God's nature. Jeremiah 9:24 says, *"I am the Lord,*
who exercises kindness, justice and righteousness on earth, for in these I
delight." And so when we are kind to one another, God finds delight
in us.

Throughout His ministry, Jesus modeled kindness and tenderness.
He wept over Jerusalem when He saw their wayward ways. He found
time to minister to the outcasts in society when they came to Him in
need: the woman with the issue of bleeding, Mary Magdalene who
was possessed by demons, the crippled and the blind. He also often
taught about the kindness of one person to another. The most famous
example may be the parable of the Good Samaritan (Luke 10:25-37),
who went out of his way to help a traveler in distress after others had
passed by. In every way, Jesus lived out His own command to do unto
others as we would have them do unto us.

Of course, the kindest thing Christ did for all of us was to die on
the cross for our sins. Titus 3:4 reads: *But when the kindness and love*
of God our Savior appeared, he saved us, not because of righteous things

we had done, but because of his mercy. So one of the kindest things we can do for others is share what Christ did for us and open the door for them to know of His salvation and mercy, too.

The random acts of kindness we perform are outward demonstrations of our willingness to "be kind to one another." Later in life, it may be difficult to drop off a bouquet of flowers or bake a pie for a neighbor, but there are smaller things we can do. If we hold the door for the person behind us, pass on the last dessert so someone else can have it, or simply offer a smile to someone having a bad day, we are demonstrating kindness. God will be delighted to see it!

FOR REFLECTION OR DISCUSSION

- Have you ever considered that perhaps being kind to others is your assignment from God?
- What do you think stops us from being kind to others?
- How has the Lord been kind to you in your lifetime? Have you thanked Him for His kindness?

A THOUGHT TO SHARE

Kindness is contagious. Start being kinder to others and see what a difference it makes!

SUGGESTION FOR THE WEEK

The most effective acts of kindness are often anonymous ones. Do something nice for someone without telling them it was you who did it. You will both be blessed.

SUGGESTED HYMNS

- O Master, Let Me Walk with Thee
- O, How I Love Jesus

PRAYER REQUESTS AND CLOSING PRAYER

LESSON 13
Trusting in the Lord

KEY VERSE

*Those who know your name will trust in you, for you, Lord,
have never forsaken those who seek you.*
PSALM 9:10

OPENING PRAYER

DEAR LORD, HOW COMMON IT IS for us to put our trust in people
and things that disappoint us. Teach us to trust in You, Lord. Give us
a deeper understanding of Your trustworthiness, and the peace that
comes from knowing that trust in You is never misplaced trust. In
Your name we pray, amen.

INTRODUCTION

Trust is key to the success of any relationship, isn't it? We can't
stay married very long to someone we don't trust, and even lasting
friendships are usually based on trust. In times of physical illness or
when we are facing the trials and challenges of aging, it's important
that we find doctors, nurses, and caregivers whom we can trust—
people who, through their actions, have proven time and again that
we can depend on them.

Even advertisers and politicians play off our desire to develop a
trust relationship. When we don't trust someone, we probably are not
going to do business with them, and we certainly won't vote them
into office. Pollsters are constantly asking voters whether they trust
a certain candidate. Why? Because they see it as a key indicator of

whether that candidate will succeed or fail. We want leaders in whom we can trust. That will never change whatever the political climate.

Yet as important as it is for us to trust in others, it is even more important that others can trust in us. We want to be people whose word is always good. People who speak the truth, and can be counted on to follow up on promises made. We want to be trustworthy.

As in all areas of our life, we can look to the Lord for the perfect model of trustworthiness. He never changes. His Word is always good. His truth is everlasting. There is a reason our country imprints its coins with "In God We Trust," as controversial as that may be in some circles. There is simply no other place our trust can be as well placed.

For Reflection or Discussion

- How do you determine whether a person is trustworthy?
- How important is it to you to be a person others can trust?
- What happens when trust is broken in a relationship?

Scriptures and Quotes

*Some trust in chariots and some in horses, but we trust
in the name of the Lord our God.*
PSALM 20:7

*Blessed is the man who makes the Lord his trust, who does not
look to the proud, to those who turn aside to false gods.*
PSALM 40:4

*In God, whose word I praise, in God I trust; I will not be afraid.
What can mortal man do to me?*
PSALM 56:4

*Trust in the Lord with all your heart and lean not on your own
understanding; in all your ways acknowledge him,
and he will make your paths straight.*
PROVERBS 3:5-6

"Do not let your hearts be troubled. Trust in God; trust also in me."
JOHN 14:1

We trust as we love, and where we love.—If we love Christ much,
surely we shall trust Him much.
THOMAS BENTON BROOKS

Don't try to hold God's hand; let Him hold yours.
Let Him do the holding, and you the trusting.[21]
HAMMER WILLIAM WEBB-PEPLOE

MEDITATION

While we may quite willingly trust in the Lord on days when
things are going well, it's in times of crisis that our faith and our trust
are sometimes challenged. Oswald Chambers wrote, "There are stages
in life when there is no storm, no crisis, when we do our human best;
it is when a crisis arises that we instantly reveal upon whom we rely.
If we have been learning to worship God and to trust Him, the crisis
will reveal that we will go to the breaking point and not break in our
confidence in Him." [22]

Can we trust in the Lord when everything in our life changes?
Yes, because He never changes. Can we trust in Him in times of
illness or despair? Yes, for He is able to heal us or comfort us. Most
importantly, can we trust His promises that once our time on this
earth is over, He will deliver us into eternal life with Him? Undeniably
so. Isaiah 30:15 reads *in quietness and trust is your strength*. In times
of uncertainty, do we panic, or do we quietly trust that God has
everything under control—even when we can't see what He is doing?

The Holy Bible, from beginning to end, is not just history, it
is His story, the story of how a loving God created His people to
worship Him and trust in Him. No matter how often the Israelites
turned away to follow false gods, the Lord always took them back
and restored His relationship with them. So intent was He on having
a relationship with us, that He sent His Son to die for our sins so
that those who believe in Him will be forgiven of their sins and have
eternal life in relationship with the Lord God. The glorious truth of

this gospel message is one we can trust—now and forever. It is *the hope of glory* (Colossians 1:27) to which we cling.

For Reflection or Discussion

- Have you come to trust in the Lord more, or less, as you have gotten older?
- What fears may be keeping you from having complete trust in the Lord now?
- We usually trust those with whom we have a long history of close relationship. How has the Lord "been there" for you in the past?

A Thought to Share

You may trust the Lord too little, but you can never trust Him too much.

Suggestion for the Week

Is there some area of your life where you are not trusting in the Lord? If you aren't sure, ask the Lord to reveal this area to you. Then make a conscious effort to turn it over to Him, and to trust Him with the outcome!

Suggested Hymns

- 'Tis So Sweet to Trust in Jesus
- Trust and Obey
- Leaning on the Everlasting Arms

Prayer Requests and Closing Prayer

LESSON 14
Choose Joy

KEY VERSE

*"I have told you this so that my joy may be in you
and that your joy may be complete."*
JOHN 15:11

OPENING PRAYER

LORD, OF ALL THE GIFTS YOU'VE GIVEN US, surely to be filled with
the joy of knowing You is one of the greatest. Help us to see all the
sources of joy around us. Give us the strength, and the hope, to bring
joy into the lives of those with whom we come in contact. We want to
choose joy, Lord. In Your name we pray, amen.

INTRODUCTION

The search for happiness sometimes demands all we can give it.
Throughout our lives, we often set goals and make choices based on
whether we feel they will make us happy. However, happiness, even at
its giddy best, is fleeting, isn't it? It's dependent on circumstances we
can't control, and it's as unpredictable as the weather. We feel happy
when things are going well, but we feel frustrated when the day is
fraught with problems. In contrast, true joy is permanent. It is joy
that keeps us moving steadily forward through all the ups and downs
of life, not happiness.

One wintry day a woman went walking in her neighborhood.
She had a lot on her mind and kept her eyes down to make sure she
didn't slip on an icy spot on the sidewalk. Still, taking the same route
home a while later, she was surprised to see a large Christmas display

spelling out the word JOY in three-foot high letters in one of the yards she had walked by earlier. She had literally almost missed the JOY that was right there for her to see.

To have a joyful heart is to have a heart that meets suffering with hope, failure with grace, and sin with forgiveness. Deep, abiding joy comes from knowing that we have the promise of eternal life.

Are we missing the joy in our lives because we are only thinking about being happy? The next time someone asks, "Are you happy?" think about responding, "Sometimes I'm happy, sometimes I'm sad, but I'm always joyful."

For Reflection or Discussion

- When was the last time you felt really happy? What made you feel that way?
- Share some of the happiest days of your life.
- Can you feel joyful, even if you aren't happy at the moment?

Scriptures and Quotes

Do not grieve, for the joy of the Lord is your strength.
Nehemiah 8:10

When anxiety was great within me,
your consolation brought joy to my soul.
Psalm 94:19

But the fruit of the Spirit is love, joy, peace, patience,
kindness, goodness, faithfulness, gentleness and self-control.
Against such things there is no law.
Galatians 5:22-23

Rejoice in the Lord always. I will say it again: Rejoice!
Philippians 4:4

*Consider it pure joy, my brothers, whenever you face
trials of many kinds, because you know that the testing
of your faith develops perseverance.*
JAMES 1:2-3

*In a thousand ways He makes this offer of union with Himself
to every believer. But all do not say "Yes" to Him. Other loves
and other interests seem to them too precious to be cast aside.
They do not miss of Heaven because of this.
But they miss an unspeakable present joy.*[23]
HANNAH WHITALL SMITH

*If you have no joy in your religion,
there's a leak in your Christianity somewhere.*[24]
W.A. "BILLY" SUNDAY

MEDITATION

Theologian and pastor Henri Nouwen wrote, "Joy and hope are never separate. I have never met a hopeful person who was depressed or a joyful person who had lost hope." [25] When we choose joy, then, it's based on the hope we have that there is more to this life than what we see. It's based on the faith we have that God is in control, and that He will work all things together for our good. It's based on the faith described in Hebrews 11:1 (KJV) as *the substance of things hoped for, the evidence of things not seen.*

So knowing all this, and believing it, why do we let circumstances rob us of the joy the Lord has promised us is ours to claim? Can we choose joy in the face of another series of medical tests? Can we choose joy when the days seem long and the nights seem lonely? To do so is to say, I hope, I believe, and I will be joyful!

Before we can bring joy into the lives of others, we have to possess it ourselves. And once we have true joy in our souls, it can never be taken away from us. Circumstances can't eat away at our joy. Grumpy people can't put a dent in our joy. No, our joy is permanent and eternal because it is the joy of our relationship with the Lord and because it is based not on what is temporal, but on what is eternal.

We have a choice to make in this life. Because we have hope, we can choose joy!

For Reflection or Discussion

- What does Jesus mean when He says in John 15:11 that He wants our joy to be complete?
- What keeps us from embracing and choosing a life of joy?
- How would you explain to someone how joy is different from happiness?

A Thought to Share

We can't all be happy, but we can all be joyful.

Suggestion for the Week

Be on the alert for a situation that would normally cause you to grumble and despair, then choose joy instead. If someone asks you about your joyful response, be ready to tell them the Source of it all.

Suggested Hymns

- Joyful, Joyful, We Adore Thee
- How Great Our Joy!

Prayer Requests and Closing Prayer

LESSON 15
Confession of Sin

KEY VERSE

If we claim to be without sin, we deceive ourselves and the truth is not in us. If we confess our sins, he is faithful and just and will forgive us our sins and purify us from all unrighteousness.
1 JOHN 1:8-9

OPENING PRAYER

LORD, HOW GRATEFUL WE ARE that we don't have to carry the burden of sin any longer than it takes us to come to You and ask for Your forgiveness. Make us aware of all the areas of sin in our lives that we need to bring before You, Lord. In Your name we pray, amen.

INTRODUCTION

Most people don't particularly like to talk about their sin—but the Bible assures us all people sin. Our sins may be major offenses, those in the "top ten" listed in the Ten Commandments, or they may be more subtle and less well-known than those. They may be the sort of sins that doesn't draw a lot of attention to us, and doesn't force us to deal with them, but that affects our peace of mind and purity of heart just the same.

The well-known Bible teacher Beth Moore tells a funny story about arriving at her church one Sunday morning at the same time another teacher pulled into the parking lot. She said this man is always on fire for God. That morning he suggested that they should both repent of their sins as they walked into church. She thought it was pretty funny that he said, "You go first, Beth!"

But sin is no laughing matter. The closer we grow to the Lord the sooner we recognize sin in our lives—and the sooner we want to deal with it. We all tend to sin in the same ways over and over, so it's good the Holy Spirit is willing to point out our sin so we are able to catch ourselves before things get out of hand.

Because all men and women are created in the image of God, even nonbelievers have a conscience and the ability to differentiate right from wrong. God is righteous and just. We will never be as righteous and just as He is, but since we are created in His image, we have a conscience. "Let your conscience be your guide," is more than a platitude. It really can lead us to the confession of sin that cleanses us and heals us.

For Reflection or Discussion

- How do we know when something we have said or done is sinful in God's eyes?
- We all know that things like murder and thievery are sins, but what are some of the more subtle sins that creep into our daily lives?
- What happens when we try to sweep our sins under the carpet instead of confessing them to God?

Scriptures and Quotes

Create in me a pure heart, O God,
and renew a steadfast spirit within me.
Psalm 51:10

As far as the east is from the west, so far has
he removed our transgressions from us.
Psalm 103:12

"I, even I, am he who blots out your transgressions,
for my own sake, and remembers your sins no more."
Isaiah 43:25

For all have sinned and fall short of the glory of God, and are justified
freely by his grace through the redemption that came by Christ Jesus.
ROMANS 3:23
For the wages of sin is death, but the gift of God is
eternal life in Christ Jesus our Lord.
ROMANS 6:23

The recognition of sin is the beginning of salvation.
MARTIN LUTHER

No sin is small. No grain of sand is small in the mechanism of a watch.
JEREMY TAYLOR

MEDITATION

What we need to remember is that all sin is the same in God's
eyes. He hates all sin because it separates us from Him. God is holy
and cannot have sin in His presence. That's why we needed a Savior
to die for our sins and make us to be without sin in the eyes of
God. Once we confess our sins, God forgives us, and we can be in
fellowship with Him forever. What a beautiful plan that is!

Some religions encourage a regular, formal confession of sin in
order to make sure we are right before God. But God is interested
in the confession of every contrite heart, no matter how or when the
confession is made. It takes a humble spirit to realize we have been
wrong in our thoughts or our actions. The freedom we receive for
acknowledging our mistakes lessens the pain of the humility. Unconfessed, harbored sin in the heart has been proven to cause not only
a bitter spirit in people, but physical illness as well. In that regard,
confession truly is good for the soul *and* the body.

King David in the Bible was a man whose sins were on display
for everyone to see. Not only did he lust after another man's wife,
Bathsheba, he arranged for her husband to die in battle so his wife
could be his! But David also was a man who faced up to his sins and
asked God for forgiveness. In spite of everything he did, God called
David *a man after my own heart* (1 Samuel 13:14, Acts 13:22).

Surely we, too, can get right with God! He hears us when we
come to Him humbly and ask His forgiveness for all our sins, past,

present and future. When we ask Him to make us more aware of our sins so we can be sure we have confessed them all, He will do that, too. And not only does He forgive our sins, but He forgets them. Then He gives us a fresh new spirit; a new heart to go forth and do His will unshackled by the burden of sin. This is a gift worth accepting.

For Reflection or Discussion

- What is it that keeps us from confessing our sins?
- Why do you think we are so much better at seeing the sins of others than our own sins?
- Is there any sin in your life now that you would like to confess?

A Thought to Share

We need to turn our eyes inward to our own sin rather than outward to the sins of others.

Suggestion for the Week

If you have been short or abrupt with someone this week, or even said something unkind about them, consider confessing your sin to God *and* to them, and asking for forgiveness. You may be surprised by the close relationship that could develop.

Suggested Hymns

- Change My Heart, O God
- Nothing But the Blood
- Softly and Tenderly

Prayer Requests and Closing Prayer

LESSON 16
Hearing God's Voice

KEY VERSE

*Whether you turn to the right or to the left, your ears will hear
a voice behind you, saying, "This is the way; walk in it."*
ISAIAH 30:21

OPENING PRAYER

LORD, HOW DESPERATE WE ARE to hear from You at certain times
of our lives. Give us ears to hear, Lord, so that all the wisdom and
comfort You want to send to us will come through loudly and clearly.
In Your name we pray, amen.

INTRODUCTION

As when God first spoke to Adam in the Garden of Eden and
asked him, *"Where are you?"* (Genesis 3:8), the Old Testament is
full of God's direct interaction with the people He wanted to shape
and mold into living lives of meaning and direction. He spoke to
Abraham and Sarah and told them they would have a son even
though they were very old at the time. He spoke to Moses and told
him He wanted him to go speak to the Pharaoh about releasing the
Israelites from bondage, and on and on.

There are those who say God has stopped talking directly to His
people, but those who hear from Him today know that simply isn't so.
God still speaks to those who believe and trust in Him. In fact, He is
possibly more creative than ever in the ways He speaks to us. We just
have to be willing to listen.

When do we want to hear God speak? We would love to know what He thinks when we have to make a difficult decision. His insight would make a huge difference when medical reports are frightening or confusing. Those facing the loss of income or problems with relationships would benefit from knowing what God thinks, wouldn't they? He is speaking to us all the time. But are we listening?

We turn on the radio or the television when we want to hear the latest weather report. We turn on the stereo when we want to hear classical music. Likewise, we must turn our attention to God when we want to hear from Him.

For Reflection or Discussion

- Was there a time in your life when you are sure you heard God speaking to you? Please share that time with the group.
- If God is speaking to us all the time, what do you think keeps us from hearing Him?
- What would you like to hear God's thoughts on today?

Scriptures and Quotes

The Lord said, "Go out and stand on the mountain in the presence of the Lord, for the Lord is about to pass by." Then a great and powerful wind tore the mountains apart and shattered the rocks before the Lord, but the Lord was not in the wind. After the wind there was an earthquake, but the Lord was not in the earthquake. After the earthquake came a fire, but the Lord was not in the fire. And after the fire came a gentle whisper. When Elijah heard it, he pulled his cloak over his face and went out and stood at the mouth of the cave.
1 Kings 19:11-13

Then I heard the voice of the Lord saying, "Whom shall I send? And who will go for us?" And I said, "Here am I. Send me!"
Isaiah 6:8

*"My sheep listen to my voice; I know them, and they follow me.
I give them eternal life, and they shall never perish;
no one can snatch them out of my hand."*
JOHN 10:27

*"But the Counselor, the Holy Spirit, will teach you all things
and will remind you of everything I have said to you."*
JOHN 14:26

*"Here I am! I stand at the door and knock. If anyone hears my voice
and opens the door, I will come in and eat with him, and he with me."*
REVELATION 3:20

*God speaks uniquely to individuals, and He can do it any way He pleases.
As you walk in an intimate love relationship with God, you will come to
recognize His voice. You will know when God is speaking to you.*[26]
HENRY T. BLACKABY

*If we let the Spirit of God bring us face to face with God, we too shall
hear something akin to what Isaiah heard, the still small voice of God;
and in perfect freedom will say, "Here am I; send me."*[27]
OSWALD CHAMBERS

MEDITATION

God speaks to all who believe in Him in one way or another.
All we have to do is listen. Sometimes we hear His voice delivering a
message to us deep in our souls. We know the words are from God
because they reveal something we weren't thinking and are sometimes
in words we would never use ourselves—Godly words!

God also speaks today through His holy Word. Reading the
Bible, or listening to someone else read it to us, is a wonderful way
to hear God speaking. Every word in God's Word is there because
He willed it to be there. So often a verse we read or hear seems to be
almost illuminated because we know it is being spoken into our lives
at that particular point in time. It's as if God is speaking directly to us.
Nothing we think we are hearing from God will ever contradict His
Word, so that is a safe place to start if you want to hear Him.

In the New Testament, God primarily spoke to His people through His personal spokesperson, His Son, Jesus Christ. Many Bibles print all the words of Jesus in red ink just to make sure the reader doesn't miss the fact that these are the very words of God. Jesus clearly stated that He did and said only those things His father asked Him to do and say. So when we listen to the words of Jesus, we are listening to God.

God can also speak to us through other believers. Perhaps you hear a moving sermon on a topic with which you've been struggling for a long time. That could be God speaking to you through that preacher. Or perhaps in a conversation with a Christian friend you receive an insight you didn't have before about an issue with which you are struggling. Because all believers have the indwelling of the Holy Spirit, God could be speaking to you through your friend.

Regardless of how God chooses to speak to you, He will do so. He may speak directly in the depths of your soul, through His Word, or through the Holy Spirit, but He will speak. Listen carefully, and you will hear Him.

For Reflection or Discussion

- Sometimes when God speaks it takes the form of a call on our lives—a call to action for Him! Have you ever heard God's call on your life?
- Why is it important for us to be aware when God is speaking to us?
- Do you hear from God directly, through His Word, through the Holy Spirit, or through all of the above?

A Thought to Share

When God has something to say to you, it's probably a good idea to listen!

SUGGESTION FOR THE WEEK

Spend some quiet time with God this week. Simply ask Him to speak to you and sit quietly and listen. If you don't hear Him directly, open His Word and let Him speak to you through its pages.

SUGGESTED HYMNS

- In the Garden
- Day by Day
- Wonderful Words of Life

PRAYER REQUESTS AND CLOSING PRAYER

NOTES

LESSON 17
God Is Near

KEY VERSE

Come near to God and he will come near to you.
JAMES 4:8

OPENING PRAYER

Lord, we know You are always near to us, but we don't always feel Your presence. Open our eyes, ears, minds, and hearts, Lord, so that we can more clearly sense Your closeness to us. In Your precious name we pray, amen.

INTRODUCTION

We know God is everywhere at all times, and yet how many days we sit and think that He must be absent temporarily. He must have gone somewhere else and forgotten to tell us, because He doesn't seem near to us at all.

Or maybe we see all that's happening in the world and we just assume that, God being God, he's probably needed elsewhere. He's probably doing more important things than being with us in the still darkness of our bedrooms. But the Scriptures tell us that none of these perceptions is accurate. When we presume that God is too distracted or too busy to pay attention to us, we are ascribing our human limitations to God, and we are engaging in futile thinking.

Because God's ways are not our ways, it can be hard for us to fathom that the same God who created the universe is always present, always attentive to our needs. And yet the glorious truth is that He is.

A sweet story is told about a little girl who went to the doctor for a checkup. Sitting on the examination table, the little girl waited patiently while the doctor listened to her heart with a stethoscope. "Oh, I hear something in there," the doctor says to engage the little girl. "Is that Barney?"

"No," the little girl corrected the doctor. "Barney is on my underwear. Jesus is in my heart." She had no problem accepting that God is always near, as He is to all of us once we have invited Him into our hearts.

For Reflection or Discussion

- Are there times when God feels far away from you?
- What can you do to feel closer to God?
- How has God made His presence evident to you?

Scriptures and Quotes

What other nation is so great as to have their gods near them the way the Lord our God is near us whenever we pray to him?
DEUTERONOMY 4:7

"The Lord himself goes before you and will be with you; he will never leave you nor forsake you. Do not be afraid; do not be discouraged."
DEUTERONOMY 31:8

PSALM 23 *(Read or recite from memory together.)*

But as for me, it is good to be near God.
PSALM 73:28

Yet you are near, O Lord, and all your commands are true.
PSALM 119:151

Let us draw near to God with a sincere heart in full assurance of faith, having our hearts sprinkled to cleanse us from a guilty conscience and having our bodies washed with pure water.
HEBREWS 10:22

Reach up as far as you can,
and God will reach down all the way.[28]
JOHN H. VINCENT

MEDITATION

In Psalm 23, a beloved psalm to so many, we see a picture of God as the shepherd of our lives. True shepherds, and certainly God would be one, are never far from their sheep. Constantly they are watching to make sure the sheep haven't wandered off, and to ensure that they have enough food and water. The shepherds take care of the sheep, and they are always nearby.

In much the same way, God is always near to us. Even when we don't sense His presence, He is there. He is there in the quiet of night. He is there in the midst of chaos and confusion. And He is most certainly there when our hearts are broken.

So if God is always there, why is it that we sometimes feel like He is far away? Most likely it's because we have turned our attention away. We have been distracted by the cares of this world or the challenges a new day brings, and we have forgotten that He is near.

How can we restore closeness to God? The easiest way is simply to invite Him into our presence: to go to Him in prayer and ask Him to reveal Himself to us through thought or emotion in such a reassuring way that we cannot doubt His presence. We can also draw near to God through reading His holy Word and hearing Him speak to us through its pages. When we dedicate time to praise God, in worship and in song, we often sense His closeness.

Never doubt that God is near. If we enter a dark room, we may not see that someone is sitting there, but once we turn on the light we can see them clearly. We merely need to open our eyes to God's light to see that He is always with us.

FOR REFLECTION OR DISCUSSION

- When was the last time you felt God was particularly close to you?
- What spiritual disciplines, or activities, help you to draw closer to God?

- What would you tell a friend who said, "I think God has too many other things to do to worry about me."

A Thought to Share

If you are not feeling close to God, it is not God who has moved.

Suggestion for the Week

Many people feel close to God by observing His creation. Spend some time this week outside or looking out your window and take note of all the marvels of God's creation that you observe at different times of day.

Suggested Hymns

- Nearer, My God, to Thee
- I Am Thine, O Lord

Prayer Requests and Closing Prayer

LESSON 18
Our Heavenly Bodies

KEY VERSE

There are also heavenly bodies and there are earthly bodies;
but the splendor of the heavenly bodies is one kind, and the splendor
of the earthly bodies is another.
1 CORINTHIANS 15:40

OPENING PRAYER

LORD, WE SOMETIMES GET FRUSTRATED with the bodies we are dwelling in now. But we thank you, Lord, that You promise us a heavenly body to come. Give us patience through the present aches and pains, and hope in a future with You. In Your name we pray, amen.

INTRODUCTION

Many of us think back with some degree of yearning for our younger, healthier bodies. We remember when we could balance a baby on one hip and a sack of groceries on the other with no problem. We may also remember running with the wind in our hair, skiing down a snowy slope, or even playing tennis or golf. Regardless of what we've used our bodies for, it's obvious to all of us that they can only serve us well for so long. Eventually, like everything else in this world, they wear out.

A woman in her sixties took up swimming after suffering with a heel problem that kept her from her daily walks for a couple of years. She discovered she loved being in the water, because due to its buoyancy, it was the only place where she still felt light, trim, and athletic. Temporarily at least, swimming was her salvation, and it gave her back a sense of well-being.

Yet everything having to do with our bodies is temporary, isn't it? Certainly beauty is fleeting, strength diminishes, and joints eventually begin to ache and pop. Try as we might in this youth-oriented culture, there is no reversing the ravages of time on the human body. Gravity alone is responsible for much of it. But the good news is that, regardless of what shape our earthly body is in, we can trade it in for a heavenly body some day! That's an offer everyone should be eager to accept once the time comes.

For Reflection or Discussion

- How is your earthly body holding up? What would you change about it if you could?
- Think back to when your body was in prime condition. What kinds of things did you enjoy doing then that you aren't able to do now?
- What's the first thing you want to do when you receive your perfect heavenly body?

Scriptures and Quotes

The righteous will flourish... They will still bear fruit in old age, they will stay fresh and green.
Psalm 92:12, 14

So will it be with the resurrection of the dead. The body that is sown is perishable, it is raised imperishable; it is sown in dishonor, it is raised in glory; it is sown in weakness, it is raised in power; it is sown a natural body, it is raised a spiritual body. If there is a natural body, there is also a spiritual body.
1 Corinthians 15:42-44

Therefore we do not lose heart. Though outwardly we are wasting away, yet inwardly we are being renewed day by day. For our light and momentary troubles are achieving for us an eternal glory that far

*outweighs them all. So we fix our eyes not on what is seen,
but on what is unseen. For what is seen is temporary,
but what is unseen is eternal.*
2 Corinthians 4:16-18

*But our citizenship is in heaven. And we eagerly await a Savior
from there, the Lord Jesus Christ, who, by the power that enables him
to bring everything under his control, will transform our lowly bodies
so that they will be like his glorious body.*
Philippians 3:20-21

*"They will be his people, and God himself will be with them and
be their God. He will wipe every tear from their eyes. There will be
no more death or mourning or crying or pain, for the
old order of things has passed away."*
Revelation 21:3-4

*I would not give one moment of heaven for all the joys and riches in the
world, even if it lasted for thousands and thousands of years.*
Martin Luther

God's in his heaven—all's right with the world.
Robert Browning

Meditation

Author and artist Joni Eareckson Tada has been in a wheelchair since she was injured in a diving accident as a teenager. After being a quadriplegic for over 40 years, she was diagnosed with breast cancer and had to undergo a mastectomy and chemotherapy treatments. So when she says that suffering makes us yearn more deeply for our heavenly home, she speaks from experience. "One day no more bulging middles or balding tops," she writes in her book *Heaven Your Real Home*. "No varicose veins or crow's feet. No more cellulite or support hose…Just a quick leapfrog over the tombstone and it's the body you've always dreamed of. Fit and trim, smooth and sleek." [29]

Of course, beyond all the issues we all face as our bodies age, Joni especially longs for a heavenly body that functions better than her earthly one has for a long time. "I'm ready to have this lowly body transformed," she writes. She goes on to say that then "I will bear the likeness of Jesus, the man from heaven. Like His, mine will be an actual, literal body perfectly suited for earth *and* heaven." [30]

While we may be blessed with bodies that work better than Joni's does, we can all relate to her excitement and anticipation about receiving a new body in heaven. Just as we trade in whatever residence we are living in here for a mansion in heaven, our new, heavenly bodies will be glorious indeed! And whatever pains and suffering we've experienced on earth will be quickly forgotten once heaven is all around us.

Do you know, without a doubt, that you're going to heaven? If you aren't sure, consider praying the prayer Joni Eareckson Tada shared with her readers:

Lord Jesus, I realize I have lived my life far from you
And I see now how my sin has separated me from You.
Please come into my life—my heart, mind, and spirit—
And make me the person You want me to be.
Forgive me for living away from You all these years
And help me to turn from my old ways
To Your new and righteous ways.
I invite You to be Lord of my life
And thank You for the difference You will make.
Amen.[31]

For Reflection or Discussion

- If you asked Jesus to be Lord of your life today, consider sharing your important step with the group so we can pray with you.
- Do you spend any time dreaming about your heavenly body and wondering what it will be like? What are your thoughts and hopes?
- Does trusting in the knowledge that you will have a new body in heaven make it easier to deal with the failings of the earthly one you have now? Why or why not?

A Thought to Share

The next time people complain to you about something that is wrong with their bodies, remind them they can trade them in for heavenly ones some day!

Suggestion for the Week

Spend some time in prayer thanking God for all the parts of your body that still work well. Then thank Him that someday you'll trade your whole body in for a heavenly model with an unlimited warranty.

Suggested Hymns

- When We All Get to Heaven
- I'll Fly Away
- When the Roll is Called Up Yonder

Prayer Requests and Closing Prayer

NOTES

LESSON 19
Being in the World

KEY VERSE

"If you belonged to the world, it would love you as its own. As it is, you do not belong to the world, but I have chosen you out of the world."
JOHN 15:19

OPENING PRAYER

O LORD, SOMETIMES THIS WORLD really seems to get to us. We become so weary with all the consequences of living in a fallen world, a world where Your ways are not always respected or supported. Encourage us, Lord. For we know that although we are to live joyfully and gratefully in this world until You take us out of it, this world is not our final home. In Your name we pray, amen.

INTRODUCTION

Every so often, someone decides that they know the date the world as we know it will end. Of course, no one can truly know when the world will end, but all around us we see signs that the "end times" may be approaching. We can't turn on a newscast without hearing about wars and rumors of wars. We hear of the devastation of earthquakes, tsunamis, and tornados. And the evil doings of men and women caught up in their own selfish schemes sometimes make us wonder if it will all end sooner rather than later.

Fortunately for Christians, we have God's promise that this world isn't all there is. No matter how bad things get in the world, the state in which we live, or the city we call home, we can stay strong knowing that while we are to be a part of this world, we are not subject to it.

Since we are citizens of this world until we become citizens of heaven, we are to make every effort to leave our little corner of the world a bit better than we found it. Yet we can also take comfort in knowing that the world as we know it is ultimately in God's hands. He created it, and only He can decide what happens in it and when and how it will end.

Rather than letting being in the world discourage us, we need to trust in God's sovereignty. Whatever happens He allows, and He has the whole world in His hands.

For Reflection or Discussion

- Were there times in your life when you felt the world was too much for you? How did you choose to get through those times?
- What do you do when you need to take a break from the disappointments and heartache in this world?
- Do you consider yourself a citizen of this world, a citizen of heaven, or both?

Scriptures and Quotes

"You are the light of the world."
Matthew 5:14

"In this world you will have trouble. But take heart!
I have overcome the world."
John 16:33

For though we live in the world, we do not wage war as the world does.
The weapons we fight with are not the weapons of the world.
2 Corinthians 10:3-4

For we brought nothing into the world, and we can take nothing out of it.
1 Timothy 6:7

Do not love the world or anything in the world. If anyone
loves the world, the love of the Father is not in him... The world

*and its desires pass away, but the man who does the will
of God lives forever.*
1 JOHN 2:15,17

*An average view of the Christian life is that it means
deliverance from trouble. It is deliverance in trouble,
which is very different.*[32]
OSWALD CHAMBERS

*The ship's place is in the sea, but God pity the ship when the sea
gets into it. The Christian's place is in the world, but God
pity the Christian if the world gets the best of him.*
ANONYMOUS

*Glorious indeed is the world of God around us, but more
glorious the world of God within us.*
HENRY WADSWORTH LONGFELLOW

MEDITATION

So how should we spend our allotted days in this world? We are promised there will be trouble, and yet so often we seem surprised when it invades our daily lives. We alternate from wanting to exist in a bubble, apart from anything that can harm or disappoint us, and wanting to fully engage in life around us to the extent that we are consumed by the world. Neither extreme honors God.

Our goal as Christians is to be fully in the world, but not of it, because we have been separated from the world by virtue of our faith. Jesus Christ understands everything about our life on earth. He knows what it is like to be in the world, for He abandoned all the glories of heaven to experience the world on our behalf. Followers of Jesus can draw great strength from Him for all the trials and struggles of life in the world because we know He experienced them, too. Best of all, He left the Holy Spirit behind to dwell in us and provide us with ongoing counsel, comfort and strength.

Yet we don't have to think of life in the world as just an endurance test! Jesus promised that He chose us and one day will take us out of the world. Because we know we are just passing through on our way to heaven, we can survive all the struggles on earth with joy and fruitful perseverance. How? By keeping our gaze heavenward on the one true God and His Son, Jesus Christ.

It's possible to bring a little bit of heaven to everything we do while on the earth when we keep God's promises foremost in our minds and hearts. We don't want to be so heavenly minded that we're no earthly good, as the old adage states. However, we can dig deep into our spiritual reserves—developed through years of Bible study and prayer—to spread joy, kindness, and patience into the corner of the world in which we find ourselves right up until our last day here. Then we will leave it all behind for a glorious heavenly world beyond!

FOR REFLECTION OR DISCUSSION

- What challenges do we face as we try to remain positive in this world in which we live?
- Jesus said we are the light of the world! (Matthew 5:14) Have you thought about what it means to light up your corner of the world, no matter how small it may seem to you at times?
- When you think of moving from this world to the next, what brings you the greatest joy?

A THOUGHT TO SHARE

Life on earth is not a trial but a privilege when we realize we are God's ambassadors to a hurting world.

SUGGESTION FOR THE WEEK

Spend some time thinking about your earthly world now. What things might you do to brighten your world for yourself, and for others?

SUGGESTED HYMNS

- He's Got the Whole World in His Hands
- This Little Light of Mine

PRAYER REQUESTS AND CLOSING PRAYER

LESSON 20

Amazing Grace

KEY VERSE

For it is by grace you have been saved, through faith—and this not from yourselves, it is the gift of God—not by works, so that no one can boast.
EPHESIANS 2:8-9

OPENING PRAYER

LORD, YOUR GRACE TO US ABOUNDS in more ways than we can ever acknowledge. That You love us enough to save us in spite of ourselves just brings us to our knees, Lord. Help us to understand the power and the magnitude of Your amazing grace. In the mighty name of Jesus, amen.

INTRODUCTION

God in His goodness sheds His common grace on believers and nonbelievers alike. Even those who claim not to believe in God are created in His image, and so, by God's grace, they know many of the same joys and blessings that believers experience. They may also welcome a newborn baby into the world. They experience the beauty of the sunrise, the sweet smell after a gentle rain, or the sun on their face just the same as do those who give God the honor He is due.

Some of these people like to talk about their "bucket list"— things they hope to do before they die. Yet it would undoubtedly be more valuable for them to develop a "spiritual list"—things they will believe, understand and embrace before they die. Surely God's grace would be at the top of that list.

Not only do we not want to miss God's amazing grace, we don't
even want to miss the glimpses of grace He places in the simplest
of places and deeds. A visit with an old friend can be bathed in His
grace. A brief exchange with someone in line can deliver a blessed
amount of His grace into their day. We must ask God to open our
eyes to all the creative ways He is sending His grace into our world so
we don't miss even the glimpses of it.

Scholars and theologians through the ages have tried in vain to
describe God's grace. It's more expansive, more generous, more all-
encompassing than we can begin to fathom! Yet those who stand in
the light of God's amazing grace know that it is the very essence of
life. It is the one thing that will sustain us throughout our lives—on
earth and in eternity.

For Reflection or Discussion

- Have you ever wondered why God seems to bless even those
  who don't believe in Him?
- If there's no such thing as a "free lunch," how do we know
  that God's gift of grace is truly free?
- As you look back over your life, can you see times when God's
  grace was showered down on you?

Scriptures and Quotes

*Therefore, since we have been justified through faith, we have peace with
God through our Lord Jesus Christ, through whom we have gained
access by faith into this grace in which we now stand.*
ROMANS 5:1-2

*And God is able to make all grace abound to you, so that in all things at
all times, having all that you need, you will abound in every good work.*
2 CORINTHIANS 9:8

"My grace is sufficient for you, for my power is made perfect in weakness."
2 CORINTHIANS 12:9

...the Lord Jesus Christ be with your spirit.
PHILIPPIANS 4:23

...the throne of grace with confidence, so that we may
...nd find grace to help us in our time of need.
HEBREWS 4:16

...lory begun, and glory is but grace perfected.
JONATHAN EDWARDS

...produce nothing unless it is fertilized by the sun,
...n do nothing without the grace of God.
VIANNEY

MEDITATION

Amazing grace! That's certainly what it is. Grace that gives a sinner entrance into heaven. Grace that reaches down to heal the sick and lift up the poorest of the poor. Grace that changes hearts in an instant. Grace that "saved a wretch like me" as the beloved hymn by John Newton proclaims. Newton, who had been an active slave trader, was truly amazed that God's grace could even extend to him—but it did! Likewise, it is extended to each one of us.

With God's grace, His unmerited favor, falling upon us we can survive most anything. In times of plenty or of want, His grace is sufficient. When we feel so exhausted we don't know how we'll get through the morning, let alone the day, His grace is sufficient. When serious illness strikes or death is imminent, His grace is sufficient. Once we accept God's grace, it pervades every aspect of our life here on earth—right now, wherever we are.

How grateful we should be for God's marvelous, glorious gift of grace, and how foolish we would be not to accept it. For to those who believe, God's grace creates a wonderful path to salvation. It is the amazing grace that assures us, regardless of what we have or haven't done on this earth, we will have eternal life simply by believing in God's Son, Jesus Christ. We rely on that eternal, life-saving grace. It is the blessed assurance on which we stand.

Thank you, Lord. We praise You for Your amazing grace!

FOR REFLECTION OR DISCUSSION

- How would you explain God's grace to someone who has never experienced it?
- Was there ever a time in your life when you took God's grace for granted?
- Share a time when you remember God's grace being sufficient for you.

A THOUGHT TO SHARE

Grace is receiving what we don't deserve.
Mercy is not receiving what we do deserve.

SUGGESTION FOR THE WEEK

If you have a chance to visit with someone who isn't aware of God's grace in his or her life this week, take the opportunity to point out a "gift of grace" you believe they have received.

SUGGESTED HYMNS

- Amazing Grace
- Grace Greater Than Our Sin

PRAYER REQUESTS AND CLOSING PRAYER

The God-Shaped Hole

Key Verse

*He has made everything beautiful in its time. He has also set
eternity in the hearts of men, yet they cannot fathom what
God has done from beginning to end.*
Ecclesiastes 3:11

Opening Prayer

Dear God, you created us to yearn for You, and yet so often
we try to satisfy our yearning with everything but You. Help us
realize, Lord, that only You can meet all our needs, only You can fill
all the empty places in our hearts and souls. In Your precious name we
pray, amen.

Introduction

The 17th century philosopher and mathematician Blaise Pascal
is often quoted as having said, "There is a God-shaped hole in every
heart that only God can fill." In other words, men and women are
innately created to be connected to their Creator.

Research shows that this exact quote may be a paraphrase, as
Pascal's writings reveal only this quote with a similar meaning:

"What else does this craving and this helplessness proclaim
but that there was once in man a true happiness, of which all
that now remains is the empty print and trace? This he tries in
vain to fill with everything around him, seeking in things that
are not there the help he cannot find in those that are, though

none can help, since this infinite abyss can be filled only with an infinite and unchangeable object; in other words, by God Himself." [33]

But whether we use the term "God-shaped hole," as so many have, or the term "infinite abyss," many theologians and philosophers agree that there is an emptiness in the hearts of all men and women that they long to fill, but that can only be adequately filled by belief in God.

Those who attempt to fill this emptiness without God may try to fill it with money, success, sports, food, relationships, family, personal development, pleasure, addictions, or adventure. They may even try to fill it by doing good deeds for others, but in the end, unless God fills it the emptiness is still there.

FOR REFLECTION OR DISCUSSION

- Do you believe it's true that we all have a God-shaped hole in our hearts that only God can fill?
- Was there a time in your life when you tried to fill this emptiness with something other than God?
- If so, how did that work out for you?

SCRIPTURES AND QUOTES

Know that the Lord is God. It is he who made us, and we are his;
we are his people, the sheep of his pasture.
PSALM 100:3

I praise you because I am fearfully and wonderfully made;
your works are wonderful, I know that full well.
PSALM 139:14

"The God who made the world and everything in it is the Lord of heaven
and earth and does not live in temples built by hands."
ACTS 17:24

"From one man he made every nation of men, that they should inhabit the whole earth…God did this so that men would seek him and perhaps reach out for him and find him, though he is not far from each one of us. For in him we live and move and have our being."
Acts 17:26-28

Come near to God and he will come near to you.
James 4:8

We know that we live in him and he in us, because he has given us of his Spirit.
1 John 4:13

Thou hast made us for Thyself, and the heart of man is restless until it finds its rest in Thee.
St. Augustine

When people cease to believe in God, they do not believe in nothing; they believe in anything! [34]
G.K. Chesterton

MEDITATION

The reason so many people go through life moving from one unsuccessful attempt to fill the vacuum within to another, is that they are operating on a horizontal basis, looking at the things on earth, rather than on a vertical basis, looking at God.

It's because God loves us that He created a desire for Him, and Him alone, in our hearts. He knows that something will fill the emptiness, and too often that something may be sin. His plan is for us to be unsatisfied with all the substitutes we use to fill the emptiness inside so that, eventually, and hopefully before we die, we will turn to God to fill us up.

The Bible carefully outlines the path to filling the God-shaped hole in our hearts. It tells us that all have sinned (Romans 3:23) but that God provided a Savior to die for our sins (Romans 5:8). In case we think we are able to save ourselves from sin without a Savior, the

Bible tells us (Romans 6:23) that the wages of sin is death but that God has given us the gift of eternal life through Christ Jesus our Lord. We can't save ourselves, but God can and will save us, and fill up the emptiness inside at the same time.

God loves you and desires to have a personal relationship with you. That's why He gave you everything you need to fill the God-shaped hole in your heart. Romans 10:9-10 says, *That if you confess with your mouth, "Jesus is Lord," and believe in your heart that God raised him from the dead, you will be saved. For it is with your heart that you believe and are justified, and it is with your mouth that you confess and are saved.*

Don't be satisfied with substitutes for filling up the emptiness inside of you. Let God fill the vacuum that He created in your heart as only He can do.

For Reflection or Discussion

- What happens when you fill the God-shaped hole in your heart with God rather than with substitutes that will never fit as well?
- Do you feel as if you still have a God-shaped hole inside you that has not been filled?
- If so, are you ready to invite God to fill that emptiness inside of you?

A Thought to Share

God created us to desire Him because He wants to have a relationship with us.

Suggestion for the Week

As you talk with others, be aware of the substitutes they are using to fill the emptiness inside them. Then suggest they fill themselves with God instead.

Suggested Hymns

- Immortal, Invisible
- O God, Our Help in Ages Past
- I Sing the Mighty Power of God

Prayer Requests and Closing Prayer

NOTES

LESSON 22
Practicing Patience

KEY VERSE

Be still before the Lord and wait patiently for him.
PSALM 37:7

OPENING PRAYER

LORD GOD, NOTHING WE DO IN A HURRY brings us closer to You. Teach us to wait patiently on You, Lord: on Your Spirit to fill us; on Your Word to direct us, and on Your plan for our lives to unfold. We can't be patient without You, Lord, so teach us to look to You for the strength it takes to be patient. In Your name we pray, amen.

INTRODUCTION

There are many things that the very young and the very old have in common. One of those things may be how difficult it is to be patient when we are dependent on others to meet our needs or fulfill our desires.

The less control we have over what happens to us and when, the harder it can be to face each day with a patient attitude. For example, it's hard to be patient when you have requested help with a chore and no one arrives in a timely fashion, or when your coffee is cold and no one offers to warm it up for you. While these may seem like mere inconveniences, they tend to add up and try our patience until we have lost it entirely by the end of the day!

Adding to our impatience is the fact that we live in an impatient world. Increasingly, our culture is one of "wanting what we want, when we want it." That philosophy doesn't always work when we are living in community with others or depending on others for our care and amenities. We even have to be patient with family members who promise to visit but then have other commitments intervene.

In short, being patient is difficult. And it's downright impossible without an attitude of humility and of forgiveness for the failings of others. What helps more than anything is remembering that all things happen in God's time, and that while we may grow weary waiting for Him, His timing is always right, and He will never be late.

For Reflection or Discussion

- When is it most difficult for you to be patient?
- Is patience a choice?
- When has being *impatient* caused problems in your life?

Scriptures and Quotes

Wait for the Lord; be strong and take heart and wait for the Lord.
Psalm 27:14

The end of a matter is better than its beginning,
and patience is better than pride.
Ecclesiastes 7:8

As a prisoner for the Lord, then, I urge you to live a life worthy of the calling you have received. Be completely humble and gentle; be patient, bearing with one another in love.
Ephesians 4:1-2

And we pray this in order that you may live a life worthy of the Lord and may please him in every way: bearing fruit in every good work, growing in the knowledge of God, being strengthened with all power according to his glorious might so that you may have great endurance and patience, and joyfully giving thanks to the Father, who has qualified you to share in the inheritance of the saints in the kingdom of light.
Colossians 1:10-12

Therefore, as God's chosen people, holy and dearly loved, clothe yourselves with compassion, kindness, humility, gentleness and patience.
COLOSSIANS 3:12

The Lord is not slow in keeping his promise, as some understand slowness. He is patient with you, not wanting anyone to perish, but everyone to come to repentance.
2 PETER 3:9

The principle part of faith is patience.
GEORGE MACDONALD

MEDITATION

The reason many people find patience so hard to achieve is because patience is a fruit of the Spirit (Galatians 5:22-23). In other words, we can only be patient once we have allowed the Holy Spirit to indwell us. Oswald Chambers wrote, "Jesus Christ does not give us power to work up a patience like His own. *His* patience is manifested if we will let His life dwell in us." [35]

Over the course of a lifetime, we have ample opportunities to become impatient—with ourselves, with God, and with others. The Bible clarifies that we are to be patient with situations that are out of our control. That sort of patience is more frequently termed endurance. But God always makes relationship to people a higher priority than circumstances. The Bible also instructs that we are to be patient with one another, since none of us is perfect. When we are impatient with people chances are we are also judging them, which once again puts us out of God's will.

We can't clothe ourselves with patience unless we are also willing to forgive whatever grievances we have against someone else. Forgiveness frees us from the sin of bitterness, and we all know it's impossible to be patient if we are bitter. So being patient isn't something we can do without adopting a few other attitudes, too, is it? We can only succeed at being patient when we discipline ourselves to stop judging others and ourselves. We have to replace judgment with forgiveness. Only then will patience flourish in our spirits and in our lives.

As we age, we can sometimes become impatient with God, too. "Lord, when will this pain go away?" we might ask, or even "When will You decide it's my time to go to heaven and be with You?" And yet we can rest in the knowledge that God's timing is always perfect, even when it isn't our timing. We can have patience when we have total trust in Him.

For Reflection or Discussion

- Are you more apt to be impatient with situations or with people? Or could it be a combination of both?
- Do other people notice when you are patient with them? How does your patience affect them?
- How could practicing patience bring more peace into your life today?

A Thought to Share

Patience is waiting with a smile.

Suggestion for the Week

Think of a situation that usually makes you feel very impatient. Practice patience in the midst of that situation this week and see if your attitude improves.

Suggested Hymns

- Have Thine Own Way, Lord
- Take Time to Be Holy

Prayer Requests and Closing Prayer

LESSON 23

Temptations Never Cease

KEY VERSE

"And lead us not into temptation, but deliver us from the evil one."
MATTHEW 6:13

OPENING PRAYER

O LORD, WE KNOW WE ARE NEVER TOO OLD to be tempted away from Your best plan for our lives. We give all our temptations to You, Lord, and ask You to protect us from them. May we lead lives that honor You, not lives that give in to the traps of temptation. In Your name we pray, amen.

INTRODUCTION

Some of you may remember a comedian named Flip Wilson who developed a character named Geraldine who was always getting into trouble and then saying in an offhanded manner, "The devil made me do it." That may be true, but it doesn't let us off the hook in terms of being responsible for our own actions, does it?

As we age, many temptations just naturally fall away. We aren't tempted by lust the way we might have been when we were younger. Success and power may not have the allure they once had for us. But we can still be tempted each day in hundreds of ways. We can sin in either acts of commission or acts of omission, so sin will tempt us all our days.

For instance, we may be tempted to see only the negative aspects of our present lives, rather than focusing on the good. We can be tempted to "give up" when it comes to the exercise and activity that can keep us healthy and strong into our later years. We can be tempted to use cruel words rather than kind ones, or to condone or spread gossip. And we can certainly be tempted to adopt a grouchy attitude that drives people away from us rather than a joyful spirit that draws them closer.

As long as we live, something will tempt us, even if it's a second piece of banana cream pie or skipping our medication. Don't think the evil one has lost interest in tempting you just because the temptations have changed. Be alert and ready to take on temptation however it appears!

For Reflection or Discussion

- What things that tempted you in the past have no power over you now?
- Are you aware of any new temptations in your life at your present age?
- What helps you stand up to temptations when they arise?

Scriptures and Quotes

> *"Watch and pray so that you will not fall into temptation. The spirit is willing, but the body is weak."*
> Matthew 26:41

> *"Why are you sleeping?" he asked them. "Get up and pray so that that you will not fall into temptation."*
> Luke 22:46

> *And God is faithful; he will not let you be tempted beyond what you can bear. But when you are tempted, he will also provide a way out so that you can stand up under it.*
> 1 Corinthians 10:13

> *For we do not have a high priest who is unable to sympathize with our weaknesses, but we have one who has been tempted in every way, just as we are—yet was without sin.*
> Hebrews 4:15

Blessed is the man who perseveres under trial, because when
he has stood the test, he will receive the crown of life that
God has promised to those who love him.
JAMES 1:12

Do today's duty, fight today's temptation; and do not weaken
and distract yourself by looking forward to things which you cannot see,
and could not understand if you saw them.
CHARLES KINGSLEY

God is better served in resisting a temptation to evil
than in many formal prayers.
WILLIAM PENN

MEDITATION

Without the power of the Holy Spirit in our lives, temptation and sin can have their way with us. But we are not helpless or subject to either when we call on the Lord to help us resist. In fact, we have His promise that He will help us stand up to temptation when it comes.

In Matthew 4:1-11, we read about Satan's temptation of Jesus in the desert. First, he tempts Jesus to satisfy His hunger by turning stones to bread. Then he taunts Him by suggesting that He display His great spiritual power. In a third attempt to lead Him into sin, Satan reminds Jesus that the whole world could be His now. After each temptation, Jesus replies by quoting Scripture. A defense that is always available to us, too.

As part of His ministry on earth, Jesus experienced every type of temptation known to us, yet He remained without sin. We can draw on the same power He had to resist temptation before it gets a hold on us.

As Jesus taught His disciples to pray for protection from the evil one, so must we. In our daily prayers we need to ask the Lord to first make us aware of what temptations are being put in our path, and then to give us the power to overcome them. The same power that protected Jesus from temptation when He was on earth is still available to us today. Isn't that amazing?

Let us praise God for granting us the power to take on temptations and send them packing. For once we do, then we are free to live out our lives reflecting God's glory wherever we go and to all those we encounter.

For Reflection or Discussion

- If you are willing to share, what temptations do you face on a daily basis?
- Have you prayed for the power to resist these temptations? Why or why not?
- How will you know when a new temptation is creeping into your life, and what can you do to protect yourself from it?

A Thought to Share

If you flee from temptation, be sure not to leave a forwarding address!

Suggestion for the Week

Pray specifically for the Lord to show you what temptations are rearing their ugly heads in your life now. Then take them on through His power.

Suggested Hymns

- I Need Thee Every Hour
- I Must Tell Jesus
- Sweet Hour of Prayer

Prayer Requests and Closing Prayer

Lesson 24

The Sacredness of the Moment

Key Verse

Ascribe to the Lord the glory due his name.
1 Chronicles 16:29

Opening Prayer

O Lord, don't let us be so focused on the major happenings and events in our lives that we lose sight of the value of every moment. We know that You created the moments we live, so each one has something sacred in it. Give us eyes to see, Lord. We don't want to miss the gifts You give us in each and every moment. In Your almighty name we pray, amen.

Introduction

One day follows another, and if we aren't careful, we can begin to fall into a mind-numbing routine that obscures the sacredness of every moment within each day. All our days are not alike, however they may appear from the outside looking in. Rather, each day is absolutely replete with moments that can take our breath away when we take the time, and have the heart to notice them.

A woman who worked as a receptionist in open houses for a large real estate firm spent many days just sitting and waiting for prospective homeowners to come in and look around. What kept her job from boring her to death was her attitude. She pledged to welcome each person who entered as if they were being welcomed by Jesus Himself—and to allow them to catch a glimpse of His love for them through her. She made the best of the opportunity she had to bring some sacredness into each ordinary day, and we can do the same.

When we are served a meal, do we stop to consider and appreciate all the steps that went into the provision and preparation of the food, and the faithfulness of the hands that served it, or do we just complain if it's not cooked the way we would cook it ourselves? When we are given a bouquet of flowers, do we gaze intently into each blossom to appreciate the intricate design God created, or do we miss the miracles presented to us?

In order to appreciate the miraculous moments God has given us, we have to discipline ourselves to notice what is sacred about them. Where do you see God in the people and circumstances of your life? Is your relationship with Him reserved for Sundays and other special holy occasions, or do you invite Him to be Lord of every moment of your life? Life is too precious and too short to miss the sacredness of the moment.

For Reflection or Discussion

- Have you ever stopped to think about the sacredness of each moment we live? What are your thoughts?
- How can we keep our days from becoming mired in the routine and the ordinary? How can we see them with new eyes?
- Do you believe some moments of your life are more special than others? Why or why not?

Scriptures and Quotes

The earth is the Lord's, and everything in it, the world, and all who live in it.
PSALM 24:1

Praise the Lord, O my soul, and forget not all his benefits—who forgives all your sins and heals all your diseases, who redeems your life from the pit and crowns you with love and compassion, who satisfies your desires with good things so that your youth is renewed like the eagle's.
PSALM 103:2-5
Without holiness no one will see the Lord.

HEBREWS 12:14

And I believe that when this practice of notice is cultivated in my
life and yours, we will find ourselves perpetually open to a God who
never ceases to speak, to love, and to nudge us toward a deeper and more
genuine faith. Instead of just grazing our way through life, we will learn
to digest and taste the sacred richness of our experiences.[36]
BRUCE MAIN

The miracle of mindfulness in the savoring of ordinary
life is the lens onto the sacred. [37]
DOLORES LECKEY

The here and now is all we have, any of us, out of which to
make life worthwhile and God present and holiness a normal,
rather than an unnatural, way of life. [38]
JOAN CHITTISTER

Life is not measured by the number of breaths we take but by
the moments that take our breath away.
AUTHOR UNKNOWN

MEDITATION

A pastor known for making the most out of every opportunity to bring people closer to the living God often talked about encounters he had with waitresses in restaurants or clerks in grocery stores that ended up as life-changing events for those people. He didn't tell these stories to glorify his own ministry, but to point out how God can use us even in the simplest of ways. "I thought I was just going to lunch that day," he would begin, "but God had other plans."

Does God have plans for every moment of our lives, too? We can rest assured that He does. We only have to train our eyes, our ears, and our hearts to be aware of what God is doing in each moment of every day. Who is He putting into our path who could use an encouraging word? What marvel of His creation will we be exposed to when we gaze out our window or walk through a garden?

Every moment we live can be a sacred moment when we train

ourselves to recognize what God is doing in it. We can invest our time wisely once we adopt an attitude of awe and wonder about the world around us, the people we encounter, and the tasks each new day brings. Then we will learn to see the sacredness of the moment and not miss any of the glorious gifts God has for us.

Part of growing older and wiser is recognizing the gift of the ordinary day, a day in which there are neither new crises to be faced nor new griefs to bear. Similarly, we need to appreciate each individual moment that makes up such a day, for whatever the moment brings, God is in it, and He gives it to us for a purpose. Let's not miss the sacredness of each moment.

FOR REFLECTION OR DISCUSSION

- Think back to a moment that took your breath away because you saw God in it. How can you have more such moments?
- What is it that makes one moment more special than another? Or is that possible?
- Describe a time when you were surprised by the gift of an ordinary day. What made you notice how special it was?

A THOUGHT TO SHARE

Extraordinary moments make up even the most ordinary day.

SUGGESTION FOR THE WEEK

Make this the week you really begin to notice the details of what goes on around you each day. Find the sacredness in some ordinary moments.

SUGGESTED HYMNS

- Take Time to be Holy
- This is My Father's World
- How Great Thou Art

PRAYER REQUESTS AND CLOSING PRAYER

LESSON 25
Walking in Truth

KEY VERSE

Teach me your way, O Lord, and I will walk in your truth; give me an undivided heart, that I may fear your name.
PSALM 86:11

OPENING PRAYER

LORD, HOW WE RELY ON YOUR TRUTH to be the guiding light that shows us which way to go. In all seasons of life it is Your truth that comforts us, corrects us, and gives us direction. Thank You, Lord, for the amazing gift of Your truth in our lives. May we never stray from it. In Your name we pray, amen.

INTRODUCTION

From our earliest days, most of us have been taught to tell the truth. We learned at a young age that our lies would always find us out, didn't we? Sometimes the result of not telling the truth was time sitting alone in the corner. At other times, when caught in a lie, we might even have had our mouths washed out with soap. That was one way to learn that lying was bad for us!

Of course as important as it is for us to tell the truth in life, there's another truth that is even more important, and that's God's truth. Denying God's truth about what is right or wrong, or what is necessary for us to be saved, has more dire circumstances than our youthful fibbing.

A game show popular on the radio in the '40s, and on television for over 30 years beginning in the '50s, was called "Truth or Consequences." Players would be asked trivial questions that were impossible to answer, then they had to perform zany acts, or "consequences," much to the delight of the audience. This was all in good fun, and the consequences weren't too serious.

Unfortunately, the consequences of our lack of knowledge of God's truth, or our blatant disregard for it, are serious indeed. While God is compassionate and forgives us for our sins, He is also just and so does not remove the consequences our sins create for ourselves and others. Better to know His truth and walk in it than to suffer the consequences!

For Reflection or Discussion

- Can you remember a time when you were a child that you told a lie? What were the consequences?
- Why does it come naturally for us to disregard the truth?
- When you consider God's truth, what absolutes come to mind?

Scriptures and Quotes

Test me, O Lord, and try me, examine my heart and my mind; for your love is ever before me, and I walk continually in your truth.
PSALM 26:2-3

"For I tell you the truth, many prophets and righteous men longed to see what you see but did not see it, and to hear what you hear but did not hear it."
MATTHEW 13:17

"Then you will know the truth, and the truth will set you free."
JOHN 8:32

This is what we speak, not in words taught us by human wisdom but in words taught by the Spirit, expressing spiritual truths in spiritual words.
1 CORINTHIANS 2:13

If we claim to have fellowship with him yet walk in the darkness,
we lie and do not live by the truth. But if we walk in the light,
as he is in the light, we have fellowship with one another,
and the blood of Jesus, his Son, purifies us from all sin.
1 JOHN 1:6-7

I have no greater joy than to hear that my children
are walking in the truth.
3 JOHN 4

Keep one thing forever in view—the truth; and if you do this,
though it may seem to lead you away from the opinion of men,
it will assuredly conduct you to the throne of God.
HORACE MANN

MEDITATION

We are blessed to serve a God who grants us the great privilege of knowing His truth. He gave us the Holy Bible to outline the precepts and commandments revealing His absolute truth, and He sent His Son to live among us that we might see truth lived out.

Throughout His ministry Jesus used stories and parables to teach the truth to the disciples and those who gathered around Him wherever He went. Often He would begin His teaching by saying. "I tell you the truth…" and then go on to reveal one of God's immutable truths by which we are to live. *"I tell you the truth,"* Jesus said in Matthew 17:20, *"if you have faith as small as a mustard seed, you can say to this mountain, 'Move from here to there' and it will move. Nothing will be impossible for you."* In Luke 18:17 Jesus said, *"I tell you the truth, anyone who will not receive the kingdom of God like a little child will never enter it."* Again and again Jesus speaks truth into darkness: the truth that His Father told Him to speak into a world that disregarded truth at every turn.

Because the Holy Bible is inerrant, without flaw from beginning to end, we can rest in its truth. From the commandments God gave to Moses on the mountaintop to the last words of John in Revelation, God's Word is truth. So when we read the statement Jesus made in

John 14:6, *"I am the way and the truth and the life. No one comes to the Father except through me,"* we can be sure He is speaking the truth.

Truth hurts, we hear when we are young, but the older we grow, the more we know God's truth doesn't hurt. God's truth heals. God's truth gives us the confidence we need to face the future unafraid, for it guarantees that all who believe in Him will be saved. When we walk in God's truth, we are walking in the right direction.

For Reflection or Discussion

- What teaching of Jesus means the most to you at this point in your life? Is there a Scripture verse you would like to share?
- When you think about God's truth, does it bring you joy or fear?
- Do you believe that God's truth is absolute? Why or why not?

A Thought to Share

It's good to be true to ourselves, but better to be true to God.

Suggestion for the Week

Can you remember a time when you stretched the truth a bit? If the person to whom you told the mistruth is still around, confess what you did and set the record straight. It will feel so good!

Suggested Hymns

- Battle Hymn of the Republic
- I Love to Tell the Story

Prayer Requests and Closing Prayer

Lesson 26

Passing on Generational Gifts

Key Verse

*Even when I am old and gray, do not forsake me, O God, till I declare
your power to the next generation, your might to all who are to come.*
Psalm 71:18

Opening Prayer

O Lord, how we want to pass along all that You have taught
us in a lifetime to our children and grandchildren. Give them ears to
hear, Lord, and give us hearts willing to share the truth that matters
most. In Your name we pray, amen.

Introduction

Have you heard the expression, "All dressed up and nowhere to
go?" It expresses the futility we experience when we feel prepared for
something that never happens. Sometimes that's how we feel about
our ability to share the wisdom and knowledge we've accumulated in
a lifetime. We may be full to overflowing with life lessons, but feel as
if no one really wants to hear what we know. Or we share what we
consider to be a pearl of wisdom discovered after years of living, only
to have it fall on deaf ears.

We may think of ourselves as just older, not older and wiser;
but truthfully, it's impossible to move through life without gaining
wisdom. Some of what we know we diligently learned through formal
education, career paths, or avocations. We learned other lessons
less intentionally, because even when we made mistakes or suffered
tragedies not of our own making, we learned from those experiences.

In order to "pass on" all that we've learned, we need two things: a heart that is willing to share and someone who is willing to listen. We have more control over the first than the second, but once we realize the value of a lifetime of accumulated knowledge, we won't be able to keep it to ourselves any longer, especially when we consider all we have learned from the Lord.

FOR REFLECTION OR DISCUSSION

- As you think back over your life, what lessons would you like to share with the generations that follow you?
- In what ways have you shared with your children or grandchildren thus far? How has your sharing been received?
- What do you think keeps older people from sharing more wisdom with those who follow them?

SCRIPTURES AND QUOTES

Lord, you have been our dwelling place throughout all generations.
PSALM 90:1

They will still bear fruit in old age, they will stay fresh and green.
PSALM 92:14

Gray hair is a crown of splendor; it is attained by a righteous life.
PROVERBS 16:31

Children's children are a crown to the aged,
and parents are the pride of their children.
PROVERBS 17:6

Always be prepared to give an answer to everyone who asks you
to give the reason for the hope that you have.
1 PETER 3:15

Our first and most important task is to help the elderly
become our teachers again and to restore the broken
connections between the generations. [39]
HENRI NOUWEN

Beautiful young people are accidents of nature,
but beautiful old people are works of art. [40]
ELEANOR ROOSEVELT

MEDITATION

Being "all dressed up" implies preparations were made, doesn't it? When it comes to making sure we pass along the wisdom we want our children and grandchildren to hear from us, some preparation is required. Perhaps it's wise to think in advance about what we want to share the next time someone visits with us.

Everyone loves a good story. Jesus knew the power of teaching a lesson through stories, which is why the Bible is full of parables. If we want to connect with grandchildren or great-grandchildren, the best way may be to tell a story about our life that relates to a special interest of theirs. Do you have a granddaughter who loves horses? Tell her how the Lord protected you when your horse took off for the barn one day. Do you have a grandson who loves sports? Regale him with any story of heroism you can recall about someone honorable who played his favorite sport—especially if that hero gave God the glory.

Even young people think about dying and are curious about heaven. If your faith is strong and you have the blessed assurance of knowing that you will be with the Lord in heaven when you die, share your excitement with your children and grandchildren. Not only will you be giving them a powerful witness of faith, but you will be preparing them for losing you someday. Their grief will be much easier to bear when they know you are where you always said you would be—celebrating on the streets of heaven!

Once you share your confidence about where you are going, it will be more natural for you to share the truth of God's plan of salvation with them, too. Tell them that Jesus died for their sins so they can go to heaven too—and see you there again someday! After all, leading our children and grandchildren closer to the Lord is the most important legacy we can leave.

Being "all dressed up" means being prepared for whatever opportunity comes our way to share the truth we know. It's too valuable to keep it to ourselves. It honors God for us to share the things He has done in our lives. And it's the only way to create a legacy that matters.

For Reflection or Discussion

- How can we be sure the Lord wants us to share our faith with younger generations?
- Can we trust that He will give us the words to say?
- As you contemplate today's lesson, what stories or words of wisdom come to mind that you want to share with younger generations?

A Thought to Share

No one cares how much you know until they know how much you care.

Suggestion for the Week

If you know when someone in your family is planning to come to visit you, spend some time preparing for that visit. What one word of wisdom will you share?

Suggested Hymns

- I Love to Tell the Story
- Pass It On
- Great Is Thy Faithfulness

Prayer Requests and Closing Prayer

LESSON 27
Count Your Blessings

KEY VERSE

*"The Lord bless you and keep you; the Lord make his face shine
upon you and be gracious to you; the Lord turn
his face toward you and give you peace."*
NUMBERS 6:24-26

OPENING PRAYER

O LORD, HOW MANY BLESSINGS You have bestowed on us in the
span of a lifetime. Make us mindful of the blessings we have received,
Lord, and give us hearts to pass blessings along to others at every
opportunity. In Your name we pray, amen.

INTRODUCTION

It is so easy to focus on all that we have lost in life, or the
problems and health issues we face, and overlook all the blessings the
Lord has sent our way. The truth is blessings surround us. Each day
we live is a day with many blessings in it if we just open our eyes and
hearts to see them, but so often we don't.

For instance, we are good at "hellos" but bad at "goodbyes" when
it means that someone we love is leaving our sight. But we need to
remember that children and grandchildren are blessings not everyone
is given. We would love to have them close enough to see frequently,
but whether they are near or far, they are blessings for which we
should be grateful.

Even having just enough to sustain us is a blessing when we stop
to think about it. If we have more than we need we may become

obsessed with material things, and if we have too little then we have to focus all our energies and resources on survival. So when God gives us just enough, that's a blessing!

Whether it's food to eat, clothing to wear, a roof over our heads or any of the opportunities God offers us, we are blessed when we have just what we need.

And even the simplest things of life: a bird pausing on a windowsill, a smile from a friend or acquaintance, or the sun appearing after the rain can bring us great pleasure when we see them not as happenstances, but as blessings.

For Reflection or Discussion

- Do you ever stop to think about these sorts of everyday blessings? Name some that come to mind.
- Why do you think we often fail to acknowledge the blessings we receive?
- Even memories can be blessings when we recall them. What memories bless you in this season of your life?

Scriptures and Quotes

From the Lord comes deliverance. May your blessing be on your people.
Psalm 3:8

Blessed are those whose strength is in you,
who have set their hearts on pilgrimage.
Psalm 84:5

I will send down showers in season; there will be showers of blessing.
Ezekiel 34:26

See if I will not throw open the floodgates of heaven and pour out
so much blessing that you will not have room enough for it.
Malachi 3:10

The same Lord is Lord of all and richly blesses all who call on him, for,
"Everyone who calls on the name of the Lord will be saved."
ROMANS 10:12-13

He who blesses most is blest.
JOHN GREENLEAF WHITTIER

Blessed are the valiant who have lived in the Lord.
THOMAS CARLYLE

MEDITATION

So what do we do with a lifetime of accumulated blessings? Most of us want to be more like a river than a lake. We don't want the blessings to end with us; rather, we want to keep them moving to the generations that follow. The blessings with the most impact may not have anything to do with material things, finances, or even wisdom. Rather they may be blessings from us to our children.

The Bible contains many incidences when people received the blessing of their elders. It's not too late if we haven't officially given a blessing to our children or grandchildren. Family counselors John Trent and Gary Smalley identified five critical steps to take in giving this sort of blessing. First, they wrote in *The Gift of the Blessing*, an effective blessing contains meaningful touch. Nothing beats a hug— but any loving touch will do. Second, the blessing must be in the form of a spoken message. We have to tell our children we love them over and over, not assume they know. Third, we need to attach high value to our children by letting them know how important they are to us. Fourth, we need to picture a special future for them, to let them know that we can see them accomplishing their dreams without putting great expectations on them. And fifth, we need to make an active commitment to fulfill the blessing by acting responsibly toward them.[41]

It truly is more blessed to give than to receive. After a lifetime of blessings, we mustn't stop short of giving our children the most important blessing of all—our love and approval of them. Even adults in their fifties and sixties long for this sort of blessing from their parents if they haven't received it. Be generous with your blessings, and you will be blessed indeed! When we call on the name of the Lord, and express our gratitude for all the blessings He has given us, then our salvation becomes the greatest blessing of all.

For Reflection or Discussion

- If you kept a "blessings scrapbook" what would be in it? How many volumes would you have filled?
- Have you ever intentionally given a blessing to your children in the way described above? Why or why not?
- Why is God's gift of salvation the greatest blessing of all?

A Thought to Share

A blessing in disguise is better than no blessing at all!

Suggestion for the Week

Is there someone you know who is longing to receive your blessing? Give it to them this week.

Suggested Hymns

- Bless His Holy Name
- Doxology
- Count Your Blessings

Prayer Requests and Closing Prayer

Lesson 28
Standing on the Promises

Key Verse

*The Lord is faithful to all his promises
and loving toward all he has made.*
Psalm 145:13

Opening Prayer

O Lord, how we rely on the promises You have made to us through Your Word. When all else fails, and everything else in life disappoints us, we still stand because of Your promises. Thank You, Lord, for Your great faithfulness to us. In Your name we pray, amen.

Introduction

At times, it can feel as if life is nothing more than a series of disappointments and broken promises. Because we are human and are in relationships with others who are as prone to weakness and sin as we ourselves are, it's inevitable that the history of any one of us will include broken promises—both those others break and those we break ourselves.

Don't we spend most of our adult lives looking for a guarantee we can depend on? Whether it's a major appliance or a marriage, we expect perfect performance or we are disappointed. So we invest in the stocks that promise the greatest return and the people who seem to have the most to offer. Yet in the end, we come to realize that, as Benjamin Franklin said, "In this world nothing is certain but death and taxes." Even the material possessions we treasure and that give us pleasure can so quickly disappear in a fire or other natural disaster, and none of them will be with us in eternity.

If we've been disappointed by the people and things we relied on, could it be because we are putting our trust in the wrong places? God's Word is full of His promises to us, and He has never broken a single one. It is in Him that we find the only perfect guarantee. In a sense, he's the friend who never forgets to call, the spouse who remembers every anniversary, and the investment that yields far more than expected. His promises are real, and on them we can rely now and for eternity.

For Reflection or Discussion

- As you look back over your life, do you recall painful times related to broken promises?
- Have you ever broken a promise to someone? How did that make the other person feel? How did you feel?
- What promises, to yourself or others, have you made recently that you find difficult to keep?

Scriptures and Quotes

Your promises have been thoroughly tested, and your servant loves them.
Psalm 119:140

*My eyes stay open through the watches of the night,
that I may meditate on your promises.*
Psalm 119:148

*"For I am the Lord, your God, who takes hold of your right hand
and says to you, Do not fear; I will help you."*
Isaiah 41:13

*For I am convinced that neither death nor life, neither angels nor demons,
neither the present nor the future, nor any powers, neither height nor
depth, nor anything else in all creation, will be able to separate us from
the love of God that is in Christ Jesus our Lord.*
Romans 8:38-39

"I tell you the truth, he who believes has everlasting life."
JOHN 6:47

"In my Father's house are many rooms; if it were not so, I would have told you. I am going there to prepare a place for you. And if I go and prepare a place for you, I will come back and take you to be with me that you also may be where I am."
JOHN 14:2-3

For no matter how many promises God has made, they are "Yes" in Christ. And so through him the "Amen" is spoken by us to the glory of God.
2 CORINTHIANS 1:20

I claim the fulfillment of God's promises, and rightly, but that is only the human side; the Divine side is that through the promises I recognize God's claim on me. [42]
OSWALD CHAMBERS

MEDITATION

A little book called *The Bible Promise Book* has enjoyed major success because, unlike many of the books we read, every single word of it is true. That's because it contains one thousand promises from God's Word! *The Bible Promise Book* groups verses by topic so that they are easy to reference in times of need. Arranged in alphabetical order, the 70 topics include everything from Anger, the first entry, to Worship, the last entry. Are you struggling with any aspect of the Christian life? There's a section for you in this little book.

More importantly however, is that there is another book on which we can all turn which has not only these thousand promises but all the wisdom we need to live a life that honors God. That is, of course, the Holy Bible. Within its pages, we find every promise God has made to His people since the beginning of time. We also find every assurance we need that He has an eternal plan for our lives. For of all His promises, the one we count on the most is that when we believe in His Son, Jesus Christ, we will have eternal life with Him.

With whatever time we have left on earth, let's spend less time worrying about the promises that are broken and more time focusing on the promises that will never even bend, much less be broken! We won't be disappointed if we put our hope in God's promises. We won't ever have to worry if He was sincere when He said what He said, or if He will change His mind later. When we stand on the promises of God, we are standing on solid ground.

For Reflection or Discussion

- Which of God's promises give you the most comfort and joy today?
- Have you ever shared any of God's promises with anyone else?
- In gratitude for His promises to you, is there something you would like to promise God today?

A Thought to Share

God's promises never disappoint us.

Suggestion for the Week

If you have time and are able, consider making a list of all the promises of God that you can remember by heart. Read them over several times to remind you that His promises are golden!

Suggested Hymns

- Standing on the Promises
- Wonderful Words of Life

Prayer Requests and Closing Prayer

LESSON 29
Telling the Story

KEY VERSE

Make the most of your chances to tell others the Good News.
COLOSSIANS 4:5 (THE LIVING BIBLE)

OPENING PRAYER

OH, LORD, THOSE OF US WHO KNOW YOU and who have received Your grace and mercy have such an amazing story to tell to others. Don't let us keep this story to ourselves, Lord. Give us the opportunity, the words, and the desire to share our story—the story of Your love for us—with all who will listen. In Your precious name, amen.

INTRODUCTION

Everybody loves a good story. Novels and movies succeed only if they contain a good story—a story with a beginning, a middle, and an end—a story that really holds our attention. Even newscasters and reporters try to pepper the hard news with some interesting feature stories just to keep their audiences entertained. Likewise, nonfiction books sell better with the occasional story illustration interspersed with the facts.

Children don't have to be very old at all to start requesting that mom or dad read them a story, or as in days gone by, they may say, "please tell me a story." Some of the sweetest times we remember as parents are the times when we were cuddled up with our children reading bedtime stories—or regaling them with the stories we remember our moms and dads telling us.

Are we ever too old to tell stories? Quite the contrary. The longer we live, the more stories we have to tell. Passing along the stories of our lives is a way to leave a legacy for our children and grandchildren. How else will they know what it was like when we were growing up, or how our country survived depression and war, if we don't tell them the stories? Hearing stories about relatives, deceased and living, helps children understand their place in the world. The stories give them roots, and can even provide the confidence and inspiration they need to succeed.

Of course, no story we tell will ever have as much impact as the story of how we came into a relationship with the Lord. Sharing our faith stories should be the easiest way to share our faith, because our relationship with the Lord is ours and ours alone. No one can tell our story except us, and no one can ever say it isn't true when we have experienced it firsthand.

For Reflection or Discussion

- Do you think of yourself as a good story teller? Why or why not?
- What were your favorite stories when you were a child? Did you tell them to your children and grandchildren?
- How do you think stories can connect the generations?

Scriptures and Quotes

Love the Lord your God with all your heart and with all your soul and with all your strength. These commandments that I give you today are to be upon your hearts. Impress them on your children. Talk about them when you sit at home and when you walk along the road, when you lie down and when you get up.
Deuteronomy 6:5-7

Jesus spoke all these things to the crowd in parables; he did not say anything to them without using a parable.
Matthew 13:34

*"Go home to your family and tell them how much the Lord
has done for you, and how he has had mercy on you."*
MARK 5:19

*"Do not worry beforehand about what to say. Just say whatever is given
you at the time, for it is not you speaking, but the Holy Spirit."*
MARK 13:11

*The woman said, "I know that Messiah" (called Christ) "is coming.
When he comes he will explain everything to us."
Then Jesus declared, "I who speak to you am he."*
JOHN 4:25-26

*Always be prepared to give an answer to everyone who asks you
to give the reason for the hope that you have. But do this
with gentleness and respect.*
1 PETER 3:15

*All that God has done for us is a mere threshold; He wants to get us to the
place where we will be his witnesses and proclaim who Jesus is.* [43]
OSWALD CHAMBERS

MEDITATION

Jesus was not just a man of history, but a man of story. Since
He was also the Son of God, He understood that many truths about
Himself and His heavenly Father, kingdom truths, would be difficult
for His followers to understand. So whenever He taught, He told
stories, or parables. The parable of the Good Samaritan, Luke 10:30-
35, gave them a clear picture of what it means to love your neighbor.
A parable about a fig tree in Luke 13:6-9 helped them understand
that God is a God of second chances. The story about the prodigal
son in Luke 15:11-31 is repeated today as a timeless explanation of
the love and forgiveness of God.

One of Jesus' parables can inspire us to tell our own story—the
parable of the sower in Matthew 13. If you remember, a farmer
cast seeds indiscriminately, but only those that fell on the good soil
produced a crop. Jesus goes on to explain this parable in great detail,

saying that *"the one who received the seed that fell on good soil is the man who hears the word and understands it. He produces a crop, yielding a hundred, sixty or thirty times what was sown"* (Matthew 13:23).

The Good News we have to share with others is that we have received the Word and understand it, and we have the blessed assurance that God has forgiven our sins and we have eternal salvation. The years might have made our listeners like the hard soil that can't receive the truth, or they've had the truth choked out by the thistles and weeds in their lives. Yet the story we tell can breathe new life into them.

The best part of telling our own stories is that no one can tell us they aren't true! We know what the Lord has done in our lives. No matter what else we have forgotten, we remember those times when He intervened to bless us or send us in a different direction. The details are likely crystal clear, but if not, we can ask Him to remind us and He will. A story that gives someone the hope of glory is a story that must be told.

For Reflection or Discussion

- Do you have a favorite parable from the Bible?
- Can you think of a time when you shared the story of your salvation with someone? How was it received?
- What do you think keeps us from sharing our salvation story?

A Thought to Share

History is His story—the story of God's love for His people.

Suggestion for the Week

Spend some time thinking of an inspiring story about God from your life and share it with at least one person this week.

Suggested Hymns

- I Love to Tell the Story
- Tell Me the Old, Old Story

Prayer Requests and Closing Prayer

NOTES

LESSON 30

We Are New Creatures

KEY VERSE

Therefore, if anyone is in Christ, he is a new creation;
the old has gone, the new has come!
2 CORINTHIANS 5:17

OPENING PRAYER

O LORD, THANK YOU that no matter how old we become chronologically, we are always new in You. How desperate we are for Your Spirit within us, Lord. For it renews us day by day with the life giving hope we need. In Your precious name we pray, amen.

INTRODUCTION

Just the word "new" seems to brighten our countenance, doesn't it? While the old and the familiar can be comforting, all that is new is more exciting and holds more promise.

Perhaps that's why we are so anxious to see the first signs of spring after a long winter.

First, we see the green tips of leaves pushing through the ground, but the next time we look we see crocuses or hyacinths in full bloom. Even when the bulbs have to push their way through late spring snows, we are thrilled at the promise of warm days ahead.

Who hasn't been delighted by the prospect of a new pair of shoes, a new hat, or a new car? There's just something in the newness of our purchase that makes us happy in a way the old items can't. We respond to that which is un-scuffed, unstained and shiny.

Certainly, a newborn baby makes everyone smile. As Wordsworth wrote, babies seem to arrive "trailing clouds of glory." So sweet, so innocent are they—and so new! Long before we find out their personalities, strengths and weaknesses, before we see signs that they too, were born in original sin and need to be disciplined and trained, we can celebrate their newness.

Yet how amazing that whatever our age we can all be new in the spiritual sense. Once we are willing to give up our old ways and our old self-centered beliefs, we can open our hearts to the newness of life that Jesus brings.

For Reflection or Discussion

- As you think back over all the new items you've had in your life, is there one new thing you remember most? How did it make you feel?
- What's the last new thing to come into your life, whether material or otherwise? How did it make you feel?
- At the age you are now, what benefit is there to having a new attitude?

Scriptures and Quotes

Create in me a pure heart, O God, and renew
a steadfast spirit within me.
Psalm 51:10

Sing to the Lord a new song, for he has done marvelous things.
Psalm 98:1

Because of the Lord's great love we are not consumed, for his compassions
never fail. They are new every morning; great is your faithfulness.
Lamentations 3:22-23

You were taught, with regard to your former way of life, to put off
your old self, which is being corrupted by its deceitful desires;
to be made new in the attitude of your minds; and to put on
the new self, created to be like God in true righteousness and holiness.
Ephesians 4:22-24

To him who overcomes, I will give some of the hidden manna.
I will also give him a white stone with a new name written on it,
known only to him who receives it.
REVELATION 2:17

If I keep a green bough in my heart, a singing bird will come.
CHINESE PROVERB

Christianity begins where religion ends—with the Resurrection.
ANONYMOUS

MEDITATION

If only we could put on a new attitude as easily as we put on a new shirt or blouse. If only we could have something new that never grew shabby or ended up in the pile for charity donations.

Blessedly, there is something new that never loses its newness, and that's our faith in Jesus Christ. Paul wrote to the church at Ephesus to encourage them to take off their old selves and put on the newness of a life of faith in Jesus. Once we do that, we are tapped into an imperishable source of life. We will never really grow old because we will have eternal life with Him. We truly are new creations.

What do we rid ourselves of when we abandon our old natures? Perhaps most important, we rid ourselves of the burden of carrying around all the sins we've ever committed in our lives. We rid ourselves of the guilt that goes along with some of those sins, and of the unwillingness to forgive that we may have harbored for decades. When we put on a new self through faith in Jesus Christ, we also rid ourselves of our anxiety, fears, and worry. We know we can trust Him to fulfill His promises. So we can rest in the knowledge that He will never leave us nor cast us out—no matter how old we may appear outwardly.

Many people may hold on to old attitudes, old grudges, old fears, just because they are as comfortable as an old pair of shoes. But trading them in for a new life in Christ, and becoming a new creation in God's eyes, is a way of life that brings eternal joy.

For Reflection or Discussion

- If you are a new creation in Christ, do you feel that way every day? If not, how can you restore a sense of newness to your relationship with Him?
- Not everything old is good just because it is old. Are you holding on to any old grudges, attitudes, or fears that you need to toss out today?
- Being a new creation in Jesus Christ means you are His ambassador on earth. How can you help others to experience the joy of being a new creation every day of their lives?

A Thought to Share

We're never too old to be new in Christ Jesus.

Suggestion for the Week

Focus on putting on a new attitude this week—and give God the glory!

Suggested Hymns

- Great is Thy Faithfulness
- I Am Thine, O Lord

Prayer Requests and Closing Prayer

LESSON 31
Letting Go

KEY VERSE

Jesus looked at them and said, "With man this is impossible,
but not with God; all things are possible with God."
MARK 10:27

OPENING PRAYER

OH LORD, HOW OFTEN WE FIND OURSELVES clinging to things we
need to let go. Give us hearts that are willing to surrender all, Lord. In
Your name we pray, amen.

INTRODUCTION

So often it seems like growing older is a continuous process of
letting go of one thing or another. As we see our youth slipping away,
we also may lose our roles at home or work, ultimately our homes
themselves, and many of our worldly possessions. Relationships also
end as dear friends or spouses pass away and leave us grieving with
hearts that just want to hold on, not let go.

A middle-aged woman who lost her mother at an early age
struggled with materialism most of her adult life. She also struggled
with letting go of her adult children. As she approached her fiftieth
birthday, she said, "I think I finally understand what the Lord wants
of me. He's telling me it's okay for me to love all that I have, as long as
I hold it all loosely."

For many of us, letting go of being in control is the hardest
thing to accomplish. We are used to being independent and making

decisions about our own lives, and we don't want to lose that control, even when the time comes that we may need some help.

Overall, it's good to take an inventory of our lives from time to time. We need to see if there is any situation, relationship, or attitude that we are holding on to with our fingers tightly clinched. If there is, we need to pray for the strength to hold it more loosely—or let it go entirely. After all, we want to keep our hands empty. If they are already full, they won't be free to receive.

FOR REFLECTION OR DISCUSSION

- Is there something or someone in your life that you are holding on to too tightly? How could letting go free you?
- Why do you think we feel the need to be in control?
- What's the most difficult aspect of letting go for you?

SCRIPTURES AND QUOTES

We are the clay, you are the potter.
ISAIAH 64:8

"Go, sell everything you have and give to the poor,
and you will have treasure in heaven."
MARK 10:21

"Do not be afraid, little flock, for your Father has been
pleased to give you the kingdom."
LUKE 12:32

"Father, into your hands I commit my spirit."
LUKE 23:46

Possession is an obsession in our culture. If we own it, we feel that
we can control it; and if we control it, we feel that
it will give us more pleasure. The idea is an illusion. [44]
RICHARD FOSTER

There is only one thing God wants of us, and that is our absolute
surrender. There must be a surrender of the will, not a surrender
to persuasive power, a deliberate launching forth on God and on
what He says until I am no longer confident in
what I have done, I am confident only in God. [45]
OSWALD CHAMBERS

As children bring their broken toys
With tears for us to mend,
I brought my broken dreams to God
Because He was my friend.
But then instead of leaving Him
In peace to work alone,
I hung around and tried to help
With ways that were my own.
At last I snatched them back and cried,
"How could you be so slow?"
"My child," He said, "What could I do?
You never did let go."
AUTHOR UNKNOWN

MEDITATION

When the rich young ruler asked Jesus how he could enter the kingdom of heaven, Jesus quickly saw that the man was too wrapped up in his possessions to surrender all for God. That's why He told him to sell all that he had and give it to the poor. The disciples were surprised Jesus would ask the man to give up so much. That's why Jesus said, *"With man this is impossible, but not with God; all things are possible with God"* (Mark 10:27).

Jesus knew how hard it was for us to let go—not just of material things, but of all the attitudes, relationships and desires that keep us tied to this world. God wants us to let go of the things of this world and grasp on to the glories of the next. If we are afraid to let go, we miss the freedom God wants us to have. We also miss out on what God wants to give us in place of what we relinquish.

It's much easier to let go of something we value if we think about placing it in God's hands. Is there a relationship we fret about? Give it to God. Is there a regret nagging at us day and night? Give it to God. Is fear our constant companion? We need to stop holding on to it so tightly, and give it to God.

When we give things to God, we need to remember the poem about bringing something to God for Him to fix, but failing to give Him all the pieces. When we let go, we need to make sure we don't hold anything back.

The freedom we experience when we let go of everything through prayer is a freedom those who insist on clasping tightly will never know. Just as we let go of material things, we need to let go of the emotional burdens that weigh us down. By giving it all to God, we are free to accept all the gifts He wants to give us. Everything we have belongs to God anyway. Once we acknowledge that in our hearts and give it all back to Him in prayer, we are free to enter into His presence unencumbered. Through faith, we can even let go of our earthly existence knowing that we can look forward to our eternal homecoming!

For Reflection or Discussion

- What have you had to relinquish most recently?
- Putting everything we hold most tightly in God's hands is a way of surrendering to Him. Is it easy or difficult for you to surrender all?
- Discuss how letting go can be both painful and freeing at the same time.

A Thought to Share

Let go and let God.

Suggestion for the Week

Take a spiritual inventory of your heart and mind. Of what things do you need to let go? Spend some time in prayer and give them to God.

Suggested Hymns

- Take My Life
- I Surrender All

Prayer Requests and Closing Prayer

NOTES

LESSON 32
Blest Be the Tie

KEY VERSE

*Make every effort to keep the unity of the Spirit
through the bond of peace.*
EPHESIANS 4:3

OPENING PRAYER

LORD, HOW GOOD OF YOU to put us together with other believers who can encourage us and celebrate the joy of knowing You with us. Bless us as we gather together today, Lord. We are so grateful for the opportunity to do so. In Your precious name we pray, amen.

INTRODUCTION

Travelers in a foreign country, no matter where they may be, instantly notice when someone else from their native land is in the vicinity. Bound by a common language, common values, and common history, they tend to find one another. Soon the conversation turns toward cities both have visited, colleges attended, or even people both may know. They have an instant bond because they share a common nationality.

Each new stage of life can be like traveling to a foreign country. At first, everything seems so strange. The newness of it all can fill us with fear. We are out of our comfort zones because nothing seems familiar. Soon we gravitate toward other travelers who have been there before us and may be able to help by sharing the pitfalls or providing directions for navigating the new way of life in which we find ourselves.

How good it is to be able to connect with others who have more experience than we do with whatever stage of life we are in. For example, those who have experienced grief are the best people to comfort or counsel those who are grieving. New mothers seek out the experience and wisdom of mothers with toddlers, because they have more experience in that overwhelming stage of early motherhood. Those who have suffered losses are best able to encourage others going through losses themselves. Why? Because they speak the same language—they have a common history, and that creates a level of trust and an instant bond.

In so many ways, this life is a pilgrimage. We are blessed when we find other travelers along life's way with whom we can connect. Those who will help us carry our load when it seems too heavy, or offer a welcoming smile at the end of a long and dusty road. When we connect with fellow believers in Jesus Christ, we receive a glimpse of what heaven must be like.

For Reflection or Discussion

- Have you ever been in a country where you didn't speak the language? How did that make you feel?
- Why do we find moving into a different stage of life equally unsettling?
- In those times, have you either helped another "traveler" or been helped by someone else? Describe your experience.

Scriptures and Quotes

"By this all men will know you are my disciples,
if you love one another."
JOHN 13:35

All the believers were one in heart and mind.
ACTS 4:32

May the God who gives endurance and encouragement give you a spirit of unity among yourselves as you follow Christ Jesus, so that with one heart and mouth you may glorify the God and Father of our Lord Jesus Christ.
ROMANS 15:5

You are all one in Christ Jesus.
GALATIANS 3:28

*Bear with each other and forgive whatever grievances you may have
against one another. Forgive as the Lord forgave you. And over all these
virtues put on love, which binds them all together in perfect unity.*
COLOSSIANS 3:13-14

*We proclaim to you what we have seen and heard,
so that you also may have fellowship with us.*
1 JOHN 1:3

In essentials, unity, in nonessentials liberty, and in all things, love.
ST. AUGUSTINE

MEDITATION

In the days after Jesus died and arose, many of His followers
went into hiding. Eventually, they began to meet together in small
groups to encourage one another and share their faith. Drawing the
sign of the ichthus, or fish, in the sand, they identified themselves to
one another and left messages as to which house would host the next
gathering.

Today we are blessed to gather together freely, but how do we
connect with one another? What makes us recognize other believers
so that we can be in fellowship with them? Sometimes it's as simple
as the light in their eyes, or a kind word spoken, that indicates to us
that they know the Lord. Other times it's the opportunity to gather
together for a church service or Bible study.

Regardless of how we find them, there's always great joy in being
united with our brothers and sisters in Christ. Paul, writing to the
church in Rome, said: *Pray that I may be rescued from the unbelievers
in Judea and that my service in Jerusalem may be acceptable to the saints
there, so that by God's will I may come to you with joy and together with
you be refreshed* (Romans 15:32).

Isn't that what usually happens in the fellowship of believers?
We refresh one another and leave the gathering with more joy in our
hearts than we had when we arrived. Praying together is so powerful

when we are unified in our prayers. And coming together gives us the opportunity to listen to one another, to weep together, if necessary, but also to laugh together and to encourage one another. Hebrews 10:25 reads: *Let us not give up meeting together, as some are in the habit of doing, but let us encourage one another—and all the more as you see the Day approaching.*

Perhaps we derive such joy from coming together because Jesus promises that wherever two or more are gathered together in His name, He is there with them (Matthew 18:20). The ties that bind us together are strong ties, because they are first and foremost ties to Jesus and our faith in Him. How blessed we are to be part of the nurturing warmth of the fellowship of believers.

For Reflection or Discussion

- Have you been part of Christian fellowship groups in your lifetime? If so, which one stands out as being most memorable?
- What do you see as the benefit of meeting together with other believers?
- What keeps us from gathering together as often as we would like?

A Thought to Share

The best cure for loneliness is togetherness!

Suggestion for the Week

Sometimes we don't realize how close our ties are with another individual until they aren't a part of our lives anymore. Think about the ties that mean the most to you this week, and tell those people how blessed you are by them.

Suggested Hymns

- Blest Be the Tie That Binds
- They'll Know We Are Christians by Our Love
- In Christ There is No East or West

Prayer Requests and Closing Prayer

NOTES

LESSON 33
Why Worry?

KEY VERSE

"Therefore do not worry about tomorrow, for tomorrow will worry about itself. Each day has enough trouble of its own."
MATTHEW 6:34

OPENING PRAYER

O LORD, HOW MUCH OF OUR TIME and energy we invest in senseless worry. Teach us to rest in the knowledge that everything is in Your control, and help us to replace worry with faith. In Your name we pray, amen.

INTRODUCTION

Some of us are so good at worrying that we don't even know what we are worrying about half the time. We just worry!

When we are worrying, we think about something over and over again without coming to any helpful conclusions or without taking any action to alleviate our anxiety. Worry becomes a habit that drains us of our energy and can even affect our health.

Some people develop headaches, upset stomachs, or muscle tension just because they are worrying. Over a long period, these conditions can be very harmful. Also, worry robs us of the peace of mind we truly want. It uses up time we can never get back, and it is difficult for us to keep our focus on more productive things when we are worrying.

So why do you think we get into the habit of repeating the same thinking pattern over and over—of holding on to the same concern until we "worry it to death" as our mothers might have said? Sometimes it's because we fail to take our thoughts captive or we fail to turn them to more productive topics. Sometimes it's due to a lack of faith that God has everything under control.

When we stop to think about it, most of the things we worry about never happen or are completely out of our control. Better to spend our time on the people and things we can influence than on worrying about things we cannot change. We need to leave those things in the very capable hands of God.

For Reflection or Discussion

- Do you spend a good part of each day worrying about something?
- How does worry affect your state of mind or health?
- Why do you think we resort to worrying?

Scriptures and Quotes

"Look at the birds of the air; they do not sow or reap or store away in barns, and yet your heavenly Father feeds them. Are you not much more valuable than they? Who of you by worrying can add a single hour to his life?"
Matthew 6:26-27

We demolish arguments and every pretension that sets itself up against the knowledge of God, and we take captive every thought to make it obedient to Christ.
2 Corinthians 10:5

Do not be anxious about anything, but in everything, by prayer and petition, with thanksgiving, present your requests to God. And the peace of God, which transcends all understanding, will guard your hearts and your minds in Christ Jesus.
Philippians 4:6-7

Live in each season as it passes; breathe the air, drink the drink,
taste the fruit, and resign yourself to the influences of each.
HENRY DAVID THOREAU

No longer forward nor behind I look in hope and fear;
But grateful take the good I find, The best of now and here.
JOHN GREENLEAF WHITTIER

The mind that is anxious about future events is miserable.
SENECA

Do not anticipate trouble, or worry about what may never happen.
Keep in the sunlight.
BENJAMIN FRANKLIN

MEDITATION

We may not be able to prevent ourselves from worrying, but we can learn to worry in a more productive way. Healthy worrying leads to action, and when that action is prayer, the worry will just go away. Even when we feel anxious but don't know exactly what we are worrying about, time spent in prayer can alleviate our floating anxiety and unveil our hidden worries. With God's help, we can manage our worries, or get rid of them entirely. If we give worry any power at all, it should only be the power that drives us to our knees in prayer.

Although there are many passages in the Bible that encourage us to rest in the Lord and not to give in to fear and worry, we turn most often to Matthew 6:25-34. In this beautiful teaching passage, Jesus encourages the multitudes who have gathered around Him on the mountainside to consider the birds of the air—and how God feeds them and takes care of them! Surely, then, He will care for us too. Looking out at the wildflowers growing in the fields, He reminds listeners that there is no reason to worry about what we will wear, for God will clothe us as radiantly as the lilies of the field!

We can take great comfort in the fact that Jesus knew we would be prone to worry, and was concerned enough about it to make it the subject of one of His most memorable lessons to us. He closes His teaching by encouraging listeners to turn to God in the face of worry, to *seek first his kingdom and his righteousness* (Matthew 6:33). And then He simply tells them—and us—not to worry about tomorrow.

It isn't easy to break the habit of worrying, but it is possible because all things are possible with God! Let's give our worries to the Lord in prayer and be free of them. He can do far more with those situations that worry us than we can anyway.

For Reflection or Discussion

- Do you have "hidden worries" that are robbing you of your peace of mind?
- Can you rest in the knowledge that God will meet all your needs? Why or why not?
- What one worry are you willing to turn over to God today?

A Thought to Share

> *Worrying does not empty tomorrow of its trouble;*
> *it empties today of its joy.*

Suggestion for the Week

Try to uncover the "hidden worries" that may be nagging at you, then give them to the Lord in prayer.

Suggested Hymns

- What a Friend We Have in Jesus
- Turn Your Eyes Upon Jesus
- God Will Take Care of You

Prayer Requests and Closing Prayer

LESSON 34
God Mends the Broken Heart

KEY VERSE

The Lord is close to the brokenhearted and saves
those who are crushed in spirit.
PSALM 34:18

OPENING PRAYER

LORD, JUST WHEN WE THINK our hearts couldn't possibly survive being broken again, something else comes along to devastate us. We know these things don't take You by surprise, Lord, and we find strength in that. We gladly give You our broken hearts, knowing only You are able to mend them. In Your mighty name we pray, amen.

INTRODUCTION

Many of us remember adolescent "heartbreaks" when someone we thought we liked didn't feel the same way about us! Maybe it was a crush on someone of the opposite sex that went unreciprocated, or perhaps a friendship that seemed too one-sided.

Those heartbreaks seemed devastating at the time, but the longer we live the more we realize that they were truly minor in the overall scheme of things. Unfortunately, as life goes on, our heartaches can become much more serious, and their lasting effects more devastating.

Whether we receive bad news about someone we love, or merely hear of natural disasters occurring in the world when we turn on the nightly news, our hearts can feel like they are breaking once again. Manmade disasters also distress us. We can rarely avoid things like betrayal, disappointment, and failure in the course of a lifetime. All bring with them the possibility that our hearts will be broken once again.

Those who bounce back from a broken heart, who are able to continue in spite of the pain, have the most success in life, however. Just as a broken bone can heal to be even stronger than it was before, broken hearts can heal, too. While the scars of painful heartbreak may remain, our hearts are stronger when we can remember that we survived the pain of the past.

The Christian music group Point of Grace sings about such recovery from heartbreak with the words, "Heal the wound but leave the scar, a reminder of how merciful you are." [46] When we let God do the healing, our hearts will be strong indeed.

For Reflection or Discussion

- Most of us have early memories of times our hearts were broken. Share one if you are willing.
- Was there ever a time when you thought you wouldn't survive your broken heart? What happened?
- The term "broken heart" is meant figuratively, but we truly can suffer physical pain in times of severe grief or disappointment. Have you ever experienced physical symptoms as the result of a broken heart?

Scriptures and Quotes

"Man looks at the outward appearance, but the Lord looks at the heart."
1 Samuel 16:7

But you are a shield around me, O Lord;
you bestow glory on me and lift up my head.
Psalm 3:3

The sacrifices of God are a broken spirit; a broken and contrite heart,
O God, you will not despise.
Psalm 51:17

He heals the brokenhearted and binds up their wounds.
PSALM 147:3

The Spirit of the Sovereign Lord is on me, because the Lord has anointed me to preach good news to the poor. He has sent me to bind up the brokenhearted, to proclaim freedom for the captives and release from darkness for the prisoners.
ISAIAH 61:1

We also rejoice in our sufferings, because we know that suffering produces perseverance, perseverance, character; and character, hope.
ROMANS 5:3

God heals, and the doctor takes the fee.
BENJAMIN FRANKLIN

How else but through a broken heart may Lord Christ enter in? [47]
OSCAR WILDE

If through a broken heart God can bring His purposes to pass in the world, then thank Him for breaking your heart. [48]
OSWALD CHAMBERS

MEDITATION

Because most of us suffer more than one broken heart in a lifetime, the pain feels very familiar each time it engulfs us. But with time comes wisdom and the knowledge that we not only can survive this latest hurt, but with God's help, we will be stronger because of it. It may be of little comfort that whatever doesn't kill us makes us stronger, but it's also true.

In time, we also learn that only God can mend a broken heart. The more quickly we give our pain over to Him, the sooner we will be able to feel His healing balm on our hearts. When God heals our wounds, they heal completely, from the inside out, leaving only the scar to remind us of His great and mighty work in us.

God doesn't necessarily want us to suffer, but He can, and will, use our suffering to draw us closer to Him. A broken heart is a heart that reaches out for relief and help—and the only place to find both is at the feet of the Lord. Our brokenness releases us from the sins of pride and ego, and places us in a malleable state. The Lord can then use the crisis to mold us as He walks with us through it.

Is your heart broken today? Give it all, every broken piece of it, to the Lord. In His hands, broken hearts are mended. In His hands, life is restored and seeds of hope are planted. In His hands, we can be far stronger than we ever imagined we could be, because it's not our strength that sustains us, but His strength in us.

For Reflection or Discussion

- Why do you think people fail to give their broken hearts to the Lord?
- What is the result of continuously living with a broken heart—one that never heals?
- Was there a time in your life when God healed your broken heart? How did you recognize His handiwork?

A Thought to Share

God mends the broken heart, and restores the brokenhearted.

Suggestion for the Week

Do you know someone who has suffered a broken heart recently? Show them you care in a simple, meaningful way.

Suggested Hymns

- He Touched Me
- Jesus, I Come

Prayer Requests and Closing Prayer

Lesson 35

Spiritual Gifts

Key Verse

Therefore you do not lack any spiritual gift as you eagerly wait for our Lord Jesus Christ to be revealed.
1 Corinthians 1:7

Opening Prayer

O Lord, remind us that a part of the blessing we have received from You is a variety of spiritual gifts which we can use to make this world a better place. Keep us mindful of our individual gifts, Lord, and direct us in the way You would have us use them. In Your name we pray, amen.

Introduction

We don't have to live very long before we start to notice that we are different in some way from other people. We are short and they are tall, or we are outgoing and they are shy. Psychologists have developed "personality tests" to help us discover even more about our differences. So we are given more labels to wear through life. We are "introverted" or "extroverted," we are "gregarious" or "solitary," and we are "assertive" or "amiable." The distinctions go on and on.

In some ways, it's good to be aware of our differences as well as of our strengths and weaknesses. After all, we can be more effective, and have a greater impact on the world, when we direct our focus and energy in the direction of our skills and talents.

Yet one of the most discouraging traps we humans fall into is the proclivity to compare ourselves to others. For some reason, we confuse differences with preferences. We falsely think that someone else is more gifted than we are, when really it's just that they have a different gift.

This is certainly true of our spiritual gifts. Apart from our skills or talents, we receive spiritual gifts when we become believers in Jesus Christ. Yet we need to make sure we don't inadvertently omit from our lives something God would have intended for us to do because we falsely believe it's not part of our individual makeup. Maybe we just aren't aware of that gift yet.

It takes each instrument in a symphony orchestra playing a specific part to give us an overall thrilling performance. Likewise, each singer in a barbershop quartet has a part to sing, and the result is much better than if all four were singing the same notes. So it is with the spiritual gifts we have been given. When we all endeavor to use our gifts faithfully, the result can be beautiful.

FOR REFLECTION OR DISCUSSION

- What special skills or talents do you feel you have been given in your lifetime? Don't be too humble now!
- What about your spiritual gifts? Do you know what they are? Are you ever tempted to compare your gifts to those of others?
- How is your unique gifting needed in the world today?

SCRIPTURES AND QUOTES

We have different gifts, according to the grace given us. If a man's gift is prophesying, let him use it in proportion to his faith. If it is serving, let him serve; if it is teaching, let him teach; if it is encouraging, let him encourage; if it is contributing to the needs of others, let him give generously; if it is leadership, let him govern diligently; if it is showing mercy, let him do it cheerfully.
ROMANS 12:6-8

There are different kinds of gifts, but the same Spirit. There are different kinds of service, but the same Lord. There are different kinds of working, but the same God works all of them in all men.
I CORINTHIANS 12:4-6

Now to each one the manifestation of the Spirit is given for the common good. To one there is given through the Spirit the message of wisdom, to another the message of knowledge by means of the same Spirit, to another faith by the same Spirit, to another gifts of healing by that one Spirit, to another miraculous powers, to another prophecy, to another distinguishing between spirits, to another speaking in different kinds of tongues, and to still another the interpretation of tongues.
1 CORINTHIANS 12:7-10

But to each one of us grace has been given as Christ apportioned it.
EPHESIANS 4:7

Whatever you do, work at it with all your heart, as working for the Lord, not for men, since you know that you will receive an inheritance from the Lord as a reward. It is the Lord Christ you are serving.
COLOSSIANS 3:23-24

Each one should use whatever gift he has received to serve others, faithfully administering God's grace in its various forms.
1 PETER 4:10

We do little or nothing because others seem so much more gifted. Because we cannot be spectacular, we refuse to be significant in our assigned realm. Soon we blame others, conditions or our circumstances. Eventually we blame God. [49]
LLOYD JOHN OGILVIE

Find your spiritual gift and wrap your life around it.
DR. PHIL HOOK

MEDITATION

It's tempting for us, especially as we grow older, to begin to think we have nothing left to offer the world. We can begin to feel empty and used up. Yet this can never be true of believers in Jesus Christ.

The Bible promises us that everyone who believes in Jesus is indwelled with the Holy Spirit and is also given at least one spiritual gift. Because we find spiritual gifts mentioned in four major portions of Scripture (1 Corinthians, Chapters 12-14; Romans, Chapter 12; Ephesians, Chapter 4; and 1 Peter, Chapter 4) we can be certain that God considers it important for every believer to know his or her spiritual gifting. A spiritual gift is not a talent that fades due to lack of practice or a skill that is no longer in demand because of advanced technology. A spiritual gift is something that is always a part of who we are until the day we die. God guarantees it is a gift the world needs.

Frequently it isn't until we begin using our spiritual gifts that we recognize them. Just as we are to be good stewards of the material resources with which the Lord has blessed us, so we are to be good stewards of our spiritual gifts—using them for His purposes and His glory.

By the time we reach our elder years, we may have experienced many different ways of serving others. The experiences that were the most fulfilling to us are most likely those when we were using our spiritual gifts most effectively. Once we are aware of our gifts, we not only know how to better serve, but we can make better choices about how we invest our time.

Not knowing our spiritual gifts is only one reason we may not be using them. If we are honest with ourselves, it's more likely that we aren't serving others with our gifts because we've decided that no one needs what we have to offer. Nothing could be further from the truth! As long as we live, God has work for us to do on this earth, and serving others through the use of our spiritual gifts is a very important way for us to do what He planned in advance for us to do.

FOR REFLECTION OR DISCUSSION

- A list of spiritual gifts includes: Leadership, Administration, Teaching, Knowledge, Wisdom, Prophecy, Discernment, Exhortation, Shepherding, Faith, Evangelism, Apostleship, Service/Helps, Mercy, Giving, and Hospitality. Which of these do you feel you have? How do you know?
- If you are part of a study group, what gifts do you recognize in one another?
- How might you use your gifts more effectively in the days to come?

A Thought to Share

A gift can't be appreciated until it's given away.

Suggestion for the Week

Spend some time in prayer asking the Lord to confirm what your spiritual gifts are and how you can use them most effectively in your present situation.

Suggested Hymns

- Breathe on Me Breath of God
- Spirit of the Living God

Prayer Requests and Closing Prayer

Notes

Lesson 36
Confidence in Christ

Key Verse

We have come to share in Christ if we hold firmly
till the end the confidence we had at first.
Hebrews 3:14

Opening Prayer

O Lord, restore in us the fire and confidence we had when we first came to believe in You. Life is a struggle at times, Lord, and our confidence can suffer some pretty severe blows. Restore our confidence in You, Lord, and in every promise You have made to us. In Your precious name we pray, amen.

Introduction

When we are young, it feels as if there isn't anything we can't do! We are confident we can drive across town any time we want to—or even across the country. We remember when we painted the house, packed boxes for a move, or went bowling with the family. A walk around the block was a snap—and we may have even run some races. But as we age, things that were once easy for us to do seem harder, and we begin to lose confidence in our own physical abilities.

Sometimes we lose confidence in our mental abilities too. Why can't we do the things that were always so easy for us in the past? Once simple tasks, like balancing the checkbook or paying bills, can be more challenging as we age. Even placing a phone call successfully can frustrate us as we lose confidence in our ability to perform ordinary, daily tasks.

A growing lack of confidence isn't going to lead us any place we want to dwell for long, is it? In order to live productive, contented lives we need to focus on what we *can* do rather than on the things that are difficult for us, and we need to find strength and confidence in the one Source that will never disappoint us—Jesus Christ Himself.

The well-loved pastor and teacher Charles F. Stanley wrote: "Will God ever give up on you? No! He is always ready and eager to help you begin again, to start over, and to make another attempt. He is always ready to help you persist in the pursuit of His goals for your life. Turn to Him and receive the help He so generously offers."[50] That's worthwhile advice, isn't it?

For Reflection or Discussion

- Have you suffered a lack of confidence recently? What triggered it?
- What, if anything, is undermining your overall self confidence now?
- Recall a time in your life when you were supremely confident. What was the source of that confidence?

Scriptures and Quotes

Though an army besiege me, my heart will not fear; though war break out against me, even then will I be confident. One thing I ask of the Lord, this is what I seek: that I may dwell in the house of the Lord all the days of my life, to gaze upon the beauty of the Lord and to seek him in his temple.
PSALM 27:3-4

The fruit of righteousness will be peace; the effect of righteousness will be quietness and confidence forever.
ISAIAH 32:17

"But blessed is the man who trusts in the Lord, whose confidence is in him. He will be like a tree planted by the water..."
JEREMIAH 17:7-8

*Such confidence as this is ours through Christ before God.
Not that we are competent in ourselves to claim anything
for ourselves, but our competence comes from God.*
2 CORINTHIANS 3:4-5

*In all my prayers for all of you, I always pray with joy because of
your partnership in the gospel from the first day until now,
being confident of this, that he who began a good work in you
will carry it on to completion until the day of Christ Jesus.*
PHILIPPIANS 1:4-6

I can do everything through him who gives me strength.
PHILIPPIANS 4:13

*Let us then approach the throne of grace with confidence, so that we
may receive mercy and find grace to help us in our time of need.*
HEBREWS 4:16

*God is not unjust; he will not forget your work and the love you have
shown him as you have helped his people and continue to help them.
We want each of you to show this same diligence to the very end,
in order to make your hope sure.*
HEBREWS 6:10-11

So do not throw away your confidence; it will be richly rewarded.
HEBREWS 10:35

*Living in the Spirit means that I trust the Holy Spirit to do in me what I
cannot do myself...Each time I am faced with a new demand from
the Lord, I look to Him to do in me what He requires of me.* [51]
WATCHMAN NEE

MEDITATION

Do you realize that God never has a lack of confidence in us? In fact, He believes in us more than we believe in ourselves. He not only knows our abilities, He knows our potential, and He knows He has something for us to do for Him until the day He calls us home.

Because of our faith in Jesus Christ, we must never lose confidence in our spiritual abilities—our ability to make a difference in God's kingdom. Rather, we must stay strong until the end of our lives because we stand on the promises of Jesus, and He is the source of our confidence and our hope.

Sometimes our confidence is strengthened when we look back over our lives. Then, we recall the times the Lord stepped in to help us in times of need or to inspire and enable us to complete a task that challenged us. In times of grief, He sent the grace to get us through the funeral service of a loved one. In times of fear, He calmed our spirits. In times of confusion, He provided clarity. All these instances are building blocks in the foundation of confidence we can stand on because of Jesus.

When all around us is changing, we can be confident that the love the Lord has for us will never change. When our physical health seems to be deteriorating, we can be confident that one day we will have a strong, new heavenly body! When someone disappoints us, we can be confident that Jesus will never fail to show up when we call on Him. In Him we trust. He is our confidence.

For Reflection or Discussion

- On a scale of 1 to 10, where would you rate your personal confidence level right now? Where would you rate your confidence in Christ?
- Looking back over your life, can you find confidence in the Lord's provision for you in a time of need? When was that time?
- What are you asking the Lord to give you the confidence to do today?

A Thought to Share

No one can shake our confidence when that confidence is in Christ.

SUGGESTION FOR THE WEEK

Make a list of those truths of which you are confident. Read it daily.

SUGGESTED HYMNS

- The Solid Rock
- I Am Thine, O Lord
- My Faith Has Found a Resting Place

PRAYER REQUESTS AND CLOSING PRAYER

NOTES

Good Grief

Key Verse

"You will grieve, but your grief will turn to joy."
John 16:20

Opening Prayer

O Lord, never do we come to You as desperately as we come in those times when we are grieving. Receive our suffering hearts, Lord. Restore us in those times as only You can do. Give us Your comfort and Your peace. In Your precious name we pray, amen.

Introduction

Most people spend a great deal of time and effort trying to escape grief, but the longer they live the more likely it is that grief will find them and claim them regardless of their readiness for it. Whether the grief is a response to the loss of a job, a relationship, or a loved one, it is simply a natural, unavoidable part of our life experience on earth.

Grief not only catches us by surprise at times, it also doesn't follow any prescribed pattern for resolving itself. It's been said that grief is like stepping on a lawn rake left in the yard. You are walking along just fine but then you are unexpectedly hit right between the eyes!

There is a story about a mom who watched out her kitchen window as her little boy ran over to a recently widowed, elderly neighbor sitting in the yard next door. The little boy climbed up into the old man's lap and sat there for quite a while. When he finally came back in the kitchen for lunch, his mom asked him what he talked about with the neighbor. "I didn't talk about anything," the boy replied. "I just helped him cry."

So it is that we reach out to one another in times of grief. We may visit those who are grieving in order to comfort them with our words, prayers and hugs. Or we may send flowers, a card, or take a casserole or fresh-baked pie to a grieving family. In this way, we try to use something tangible to bring comfort, knowing all along that the only real and permanent comfort must come from the Lord.

FOR REFLECTION OR DISCUSSION

- What periods of prolonged grief have you experienced in your lifetime?
- When you were grieving, was there anything others did that helped you?
- How do you usually reach out to those who are grieving?

SCRIPTURES AND QUOTES

Weeping may endure for a night, but joy cometh in the morning.
PSALM 30:5 (KJV)

He has sent me…to comfort all who mourn, and provide for those who grieve in Zion—to bestow on them a crown of beauty instead of ashes, the oil of gladness instead of mourning, and a garment of praise instead of a spirit of despair.
ISAIAH 61:1, 2-3

"I will turn their mourning into gladness; I will give them comfort and joy instead of sorrow."
JEREMIAH 31:13

Rejoice with those who rejoice; mourn with those who mourn.
ROMANS 12:15

"Blessed are those who mourn, for they will be comforted."
MATTHEW 5:4

*Praise be to the God and Father of our Lord Jesus Christ, the Father
of compassion and the God of all comfort, who comforts us in all our
troubles, so that we can comfort those in any trouble with the comfort
we ourselves have received from God.*
2 CORINTHIANS 1:3-4

*Brothers, we do not want you to be ignorant about those who fall asleep,
or to grieve like the rest of men, who have no hope. We believe that Jesus
died and rose again and so we believe that God will bring
with Jesus those who have fallen asleep in him.*
1 THESSALONIANS 4:13-14

*"He will wipe every tear from their eyes. There will be no more death or
mourning or crying or pain, for the old order of things has passed away."*
REVELATION 21:4

*God washes the eyes by tears until they can behold the
invisible land where tears shall come no more.*
HENRY WARD BEECHER

*His strength is perfect when our strength is gone;
He'll carry us when we can't carry on.
Raised in His power, the weak become strong;
His strength is perfect, His strength is perfect.* [52]
STEVEN CURTIS CHAPMAN

MEDITATION

While no one wants to experience grief, believers in Jesus Christ
know that periods of grief can be a blessing if they bring us closer to
the Lord and to our awareness of our dependence on Him for lasting
comfort. In that sense our suffering produces "good grief"—grief that
God can use to grow our faith in Him.

Much has been written about the formal stages of grief, although
no two people ever grieve in the same way, and there is no set
timetable for when the grieving process ends. In her 1969 book *On
Death and Dying*, Dr. Elisabeth Kübler-Ross identified five stages of
grief: denial, anger, bargaining, depression and acceptance. [53] Again,

there is no reason to believe everyone will experience all five stages in that order, and one stage may last much longer than others. But it is common for anyone suffering a loss to experience similar reactions to grief.

Yet those who grieve as believers in Jesus Christ have a distinct advantage: they have the Lord of the Universe as a close companion no matter how they are grieving or in what stage of grief they are. In times of despair, believers often express that they feel the power of the Lord sustaining them and helping them get through all the painful details of their loss. Eventually, they experience the comfort and healing that only the Lord can provide.

As we move through life, we cannot escape periods of grief, but we can rest in the knowledge that we will never have to go through them alone. The greatest comfort of all is that the time is coming when we will never have to grieve again. We will be with the Lord in heaven where He promises there will be no more tears. The greatest comfort we can offer is God's comfort—the comfort that is based on our eternal hope of glory.

For Reflection or Discussion

- Have you experienced God's comfort in the face of grief? Describe that time in your life.
- Why do you think we are more aware of God's strength and provision the weaker we are?
- Grief comes to us all. Is there anything you can do now to prepare you for the next grief you must bear?

A Thought to Share

All grief is easier to bear when shared.

Suggestion for the Week

Do you know someone who is grieving? Offer them as much comfort as you can.

Suggested Hymns

- What a Friend We Have in Jesus
- There is a Balm in Gilead
- His Strength is Perfect

Prayer Requests and Closing Prayer

NOTES

LESSON 38
The Good Old Days

KEY VERSE

"Forget the former things; do not dwell on the past. See, I am doing a new thing! Now it springs up; do you not perceive it?"
ISAIAH 43:18-19

OPENING PRAYER

O LORD, HOW WE SOMETIMES YEARN for the past when life seemed simpler and so full of promise. Help us focus on the present, Lord, and all the gifts it offers. And most of all, make us grateful for a future focused on You. In Your precious name we pray, amen.

INTRODUCTION

How tempting it is for many of us to live life always looking in the rearview mirror! Life was better back then, we might say. It was a time when families stuck together and people were recognized for honest labor. It was a time when life was simpler. It was a happier time, or so we recall, and so there is a great longing for "the good old days."

Yet how productive is it for us to focus on the past, and was the past as wonderful as our selective memory believes it was? Many older adults have happy memories of the past to keep them company, but a long life is not without its struggles and pain. If we are to connect with the generations that follow ours, it's important for us to remember the good and the bad of those "good old days"—to remember past times with integrity. After all, we can share as many lessons from what wasn't good as from what was.

One reason we tend to cling to the past is that it is human nature to resist change. We don't have to be all that elderly to have seen an amazing number of changes in our society. An essay that circulated in 2011 described a woman who was born before clothes dryers, color television, and ballpoint pens. Of course, she was born before personal computers, email and cell phones. As the article continues, readers surmise the woman must be quite up in years, but the end of the essay reveals she would only have to be 59 years old to have preceded all these modern developments!

We've all seen many changes in our lives that can make us yearn for "the good old days." But we shouldn't dwell there for long. God has also given us a present and a future, and that's where He wants our attention to be.

FOR REFLECTION OR DISCUSSION

- When you reflect on "the good old days," what fond memories come to mind?
- Do you think "the good old days" were as good as many think? Why or why not?
- What is the disadvantage of focusing on the past rather than the present or the future?

SCRIPTURES AND QUOTES

Teach us to number our days aright, that we may gain a heart of wisdom.
PSALM 90:12

This is the day the Lord has made; let us rejoice and be glad in it.
PSALM 118:24

"Remember the former things, those of long ago; I am God, and there is no other; I am God, and there is none like me. I make known the end from the beginning, from ancient times, what is still to come. I say: My purpose will stand, and I will do all that I please."
ISAIAH 46:9-10

"For I know the plans I have for you," declares the Lord, "plans to prosper
you and not to harm you, plans to give you hope and a future."
JEREMIAH 29:11

"Likewise, no one in the field should go back for anything.
Remember Lot's wife!"
LUKE 17:31-32

But one thing I do: Forgetting what is behind and straining toward
what is ahead, I press on toward the goal to win the prize for which
God has called me heavenward in Christ Jesus.
PHILIPPIANS 3:13-14

But God is the God of our yesterdays, and He allows the memory
of them in order to turn the past into a ministry of
spiritual culture for the future.[54]
OSWALD CHAMBERS

MEDITATION

Longing for the way things used to be seems to be a human condition throughout the ages, not just something stimulated by the changes in the 21st Century. We even see instances of people longing for the past in the Bible.

The Hebrew people were quick to forget how oppressed they were as slaves in Egypt when they grew tired of eating manna in the desert. Their whining was legendary as many of them wanted to go back to Egypt even if it meant they would be slaves again, lashed by Pharaoh's men on a daily basis. No wonder God grew frustrated with them and denied them entry to the Promised Land (Numbers 14:23).

In another oft-repeated Bible passage found in Genesis 19:26, Lot and his wife and daughters were spared by God from the destruction of their hometown, Sodom. All God asked was that they not look back, but Lot's wife couldn't resist the temptation to get one last look, and so God turned her into a pillar of salt!

Our constant longing for "the good old days" probably won't turn us into pillars of salt, but it could keep us from being the salt God wants us to be in the world. Wherever we are on life's journey, there's something God wants us to focus on now. Someone can benefit from our positive attitude, our smile, our words of encouragement, or our prayers this very day.

It can be productive to look back, to share a fond memory, to recall a lesson learned, or to glorify God for all He accomplished in and through us in the past. But believers in Jesus Christ should always be focused on the fact that our best days are yet to come! Our best days will be days spent in His presence in glory!

For Reflection or Discussion

- Why do you think we tend to glorify the past and forget its problems and challenges?
- One area where change has been good is the prevention and cure of disease. What other modern developments would you miss if we returned to "the good old days?"
- How can you use what God did for you in the past to encourage someone today?

A Thought to Share

Never allow yesterday to use up too much of today.

Suggestion for the Week

Reflect on something from your past that would be helpful to someone else now—and share it!

Suggested Hymns

- This Is the Day
- Day by Day

Prayer Requests and Closing Prayer

Lesson 39
Peace Like a River

Key Verse

"Peace I leave with you; my peace I give you. I do not give to you as the world gives. Do not let your hearts be troubled and do not be afraid."
John 14:27

Opening Prayer

Lord, we are desperate for peace, but not the temporary kind. We need the peace that permeates our very souls, Lord. Thank You for the gift of Your peace when we need it most. In Your precious name, amen.

Introduction

We could never estimate the amount of time and money people have spent seeking peace in their lives. Vacations, spa visits, and how-to books are all options tried by peace seekers. Not to mention the hours spent with a counselor or "spiritual adviser." None of these pursuits is intrinsically bad or evil, but if we are looking in these places to find peace then we may be sorely disappointed.

In times of war, there is always a part of the populace crying out for peace and wearing peace symbols. The sad truth is that, without military strength, there can be no peace in the world—and there may never be the complete world peace so many envision.

Worldly peace is temporary at best. A young mother begs her children for a bit of peace and quiet. She may get it for a while, but soon the noise of active children will return. A couple gets a divorce after arguing for years because they both just want some peace in their lives. But peace bought at that high of a price isn't peace at all.

Even older adults, whose lives have slowed down quite a bit, can sense a need for peace in their lives. Not just the peace of a quiet afternoon spent with a book, but the abiding, deep-down peace of knowing without a doubt that their eternal future is secure. Yet the wisest among us know that the only source for this permanent peace is the Prince of Peace Himself.

FOR REFLECTION OR DISCUSSION

- Do you have peace in your life now? Why or why not?
- Why do you think peace is so hard for many people to experience?
- Is there a particular person or place that brings you peace?

SCRIPTURES AND QUOTES

A heart at peace gives life to the body.
PROVERBS 14:30

And he will be called Wonderful Counselor, Mighty God, Everlasting Father, Prince of Peace.
ISAIAH 9:6

You will keep in perfect peace him whose mind is steadfast, because he trusts in you.
ISAIAH 26:3

Lord, you establish peace for us; all that we have accomplished you have done for us.
ISAIAH 26:12

"If only you had paid attention to my commands, your peace would have been like a river, your righteousness like the waves of the sea."
ISAIAH 48:18

"Blessed are the peacemakers, for they will be called sons of God."
MATTHEW 5:9

*And the peace of God, which passeth all understanding, shall keep
your hearts and minds through Christ Jesus.*
PHILIPPIANS 4:7 (KJV)

*As on the Sea of Galilee
The Christ is whispering "peace."*
JOHN GREENLEAF WHITTIER

Thou hast touched me and I have been translated into thy peace.
ST. AUGUSTINE

MEDITATION

In the Old Testament, God bestows His peace on those who
follow His commandments. In the New Testament, we see Jesus, the
Prince of Peace whose coming fulfilled Old Testament prophesies,
bringing a message of peace to His followers.

There are those today who say Jesus was only about peace, and
yet He never failed to take a stand against injustice. His rage in the
temple, when He turned over the tables of the moneychangers, would
not have been described as a peaceful event by anyone who witnessed
it.

So what is the peace that Jesus brings? It is peace based on the
truth of the gospel message—the peace we can have deep in our souls.
This is the peace that allowed Jesus to sleep in the stern of the ship
while a storm raged all around Him (Mark 4:37-41). It's the peace we
encounter in tragic situations; the peace that whispers to us calmly
that whatever happens we are still safe in the arms of God.

The best way for us to find peace regardless of our circumstances
is to do what the disciples did in the midst of the storm—turn to
Jesus. As long as we keep our focus on the particulars of our situation,
we won't have a peaceful perspective. But when we turn our eyes upon
Jesus, and make Him our focus and not ourselves, we will feel that
peace that passes understanding flooding our souls. Turn your eyes
upon Jesus, and He will give you peace.

For Reflection or Discussion

- What is it that disrupts your peace most frequently?
- How do you feel when peace is missing in your life?
- Is it possible for you restore the peace in your soul? If so, how?

A Thought to Share

Peace we find on our own is temporary. God's peace is eternal.

Suggestion for the Week

This week, be aware of times when you feel the most peaceful. What contributed to your peaceful state of mind? Thank the Lord for His peace in your life.

Suggested Hymns

- Peace Like a River
- It is Well with My Soul
- Turn Your Eyes upon Jesus

Prayer Requests and Closing Prayer

Lesson 40

Hearing God's Way

Key Verse

*Faith comes from hearing the message, and the message
is heard through the word of Christ.*
Romans 10:17

Opening Prayer

Oh Lord, our ears are tickled by so many words, so many
sounds, so many opinions. Teach us to discern Your voice in the din,
Lord. Teach us to have ears to hear Your messages for us. In Your
precious name we pray, amen.

Introduction

People often repeat a cell phone commercial that created a catch
phrase: "Can you hear me now?" We all want to hear and to be heard,
don't we? Hearing one another is one way we connect, and connecting
with others is a valued human need.

Our hearing is a valuable gift. The intricacies of the human
ear are proof once more of the amazing design of the human body.
Not only does the intricate design of bones and membranes that
constitutes the human ear allow us to hear stereophonically, it also
keeps our bodies in balance. Only the Creator could have designed
something so incredible. Hearing adds so much to life. Without it,
we would miss the baby's cry and the bird's song, not to mention the
voices of those we love.

As people age, it can be more difficult to hear as well as we once
could. Gratefully, hearing aids can often improve hearing deficiencies,

but we learn to appreciate the ability to hear anew—and we learn never to take hearing for granted.

Even when we can't hear with our ears, however, we can still hear with our hearts. Throughout our lives, God endeavors to speak to us through His Word—whether we read it or hear it read to us. He also speaks to us through other believers and in the midst of situations and challenges. We can only imagine how patiently He works to communicate with all those He created, and after each attempt, He no doubt wants to know, "Can you hear me now?"

For Reflection or Discussion

- How is your hearing? If you've suffered hearing loss, what have you done to compensate for it?
- Do you think there was a time in your life when you took hearing well for granted?
- In what ways do you hear God speaking to you today?

Scriptures and Quotes

Ears that hear and eyes that see—the Lord has made them both.
PROVERBS 20:12

Whether you turn to the right or to the left, your ears will hear a voice behind you, saying, "This is the way; walk in it."
ISAIAH 30:21

"He who has ears, let him hear."
MATTHEW 11:15

"I tell you the truth, whoever hears my word and believes him who sent me has eternal life."
JOHN 5:24

"My sheep listen to my voice; I know them, and they follow me, I give them eternal life, and they shall never perish; no one can snatch them out of my hand."
JOHN 10:27-28

Blessed is the one who reads the words of this prophecy,
and blessed are those who hear it and take to heart
what is written in it, because the time is near.
REVELATION 1:3

There is not in the world a kind of life more sweet and delightful
than that of a continual conversation with God.
BROTHER LAWRENCE

I prayed for faith and thought that some day it would come down and
strike me like lightning. But faith didn't seem to come. One day I read in
Romans that "faith comes by hearing and hearing by the word of God."
I had up to this time, closed my Bible and prayed for faith. Now I opened
my Bible and began to study and faith has been growing ever since.
D. L. MOODY

God speaks uniquely to individuals, and He can do it in any way He
pleases…He is more interested in what I become than what I do. [55]
HENRY T. BLACKABY

MEDITATION

How often do we hear things we'd rather not know about, and
miss hearing the messages God has sent our way? How can we silence
all voices but His, so that our hearing is put to its best use?

Obviously there is no way for us to physically do that—to tune in
to everything God says to us and let the drivel pass us by, but we can
be more aware of what we are hearing. No harm is done if we miss
a weather forecast or a request at dinner for us to pass the salt. The
weather will be whatever it was going to be anyway, and someone else
will pass the salt. But if we miss the messages God gives us, there can
be eternal significance.

Jesus knew that during His ministry not everyone who heard
Him speak would truly have ears to hear. He taught with parables
to make His messages easy to understand, but hundreds of people
probably drifted away without getting any message at all. That's
because God has to open the hearts and minds of the listeners first if
they are to hear His messages. So it is with us today.

Have you ever tried to explain the way to eternal life to someone who just doesn't seem to be able to hear you? You know they have perfectly good hearing, yet the words you say literally seem to go in one ear and out the other. Nothing sticks. At those times, our constant prayer needs to be that God would open their hearts and minds so that they will have ears to hear His truth.

Similarly, we need to make sure we aren't missing any of God's messages to us. Whether He's speaking to us through His Word, the preaching of a respected pastor, or casual conversation with a good friend, we know He will never stop speaking to us. Our daily prayer needs to be that God will open our ears to hear whatever He wants to say to us. Most of all, we need to hear and believe His message for eternal life: that those who believe in Jesus Christ as God's Son, and ask Him to forgive them and to be their Lord, will dwell with Him in heaven forever. That's a message worth hearing—and believing.

For Reflection or Discussion

- Have you ever heard a direct message from God? How was the message delivered?
- What is the last message you heard that you knew was directly from God? How did you know?
- What needs to change in your life so that you won't miss, but will always hear, the messages God has for you?

A Thought to Share

The first four letters in heart are HEAR.
What we truly hear, we keep in our hearts.

Suggestion for the Week

Be intentional when you are listening to someone this week. Really hear what they are saying, just as God hears you. You will both be blessed.

Suggested Hymns

- In the Garden
- I Heard the Voice of Jesus Say

Prayer Requests and Closing Prayer

NOTES

LESSON 41
Sunrise Hope

KEY VERSE

Show me your ways, O Lord, teach me your paths; guide me
in your truth and teach me, for you are God my Savior,
and my hope is in you all day long.
PSALM 25:4-5

OPENING PRAYER

LORD, HOW DESPERATELY WE NEED the hope that comes with each new day. Thank You, Lord, that no matter how dark the night, the sun rises again in the morning and we have new hope in You. In Your precious name we pray, amen.

INTRODUCTION

Few events can be counted on to occur day after day, but the rising of the sun is one of them. Even on a cloudy day, when the heat and light of the sun are minimal, we can still see that the sun did indeed rise once again!

And how grateful we are for the blessing of the sun in our lives. Without it, we would be in perpetual darkness. Without it, plant life on the earth, including all the flowers and trees that bring us so much joy, would shrivel and disappear and so much of the beauty we enjoy would cease to exist. In fact, all of life would disappear from the earth, all because we lost the sun.

Those who live in parts of the country where the days are very short in the wintertime have a special appreciation for the sun—and understand better than the rest of us how precious it is. Even those in other locations notice when the days are shorter and may fall victim to SAD—seasonal affective disorder. This condition can result in lethargy and depression. The cure is to turn on bright lights and try to create the experience of more sun in your life! We need the sun for all its life-giving properties.

Our very life on earth is marked by the number of sunrises and sunsets we experience, but do we really experience them? Do we appreciate the sun and the majesty of the Creation that allows it to shine day after day, or do we take it for granted? It's never too late to appreciate the sun—begin today and let the restorative hope the sun represents fill your heart and mind. Thank God for the sun He created, and for His Son who came to earth that we might have eternal life and live in the light of heaven with Him one fine day.

For Reflection or Discussion

- Some people describe themselves as "sun worshipers." Of course, it's never wise to worship the Creation instead of the Creator, but were you ever a "sun worshiper" of sorts?
- Do you feel like you have enough sunshine in your life now? What precautions do you take to keep from getting too much of the sun's rays?
- How does the daily rising of the sun give you hope?

Scriptures and Quotes

Yet this I call to mind and therefore I have hope: Because of the Lord's great love we are not consumed, for his compassions never fail. They are new every morning; great is your faithfulness.
Lamentations 3:21-23

The Lord is good to those whose hope is in him, to the one who seeks him; it is good to wait quietly for the salvation of the Lord.
Lamentations 3:25-26

To them God has chosen to make known among the Gentiles the glorious riches of this mystery, which is Christ in you, the hope of glory.
Colossians 1:27

We have this hope as an anchor for the soul, firm and secure.
HEBREWS 6:19

*Now faith is being sure of what we hope for
and certain of what we do not see.*
HEBREWS 11:1

*The city does not need the sun or the moon to shine on it,
for the glory of God gives it light, and the Lamb is its lamp.*
REVELATION 21:23

*Hope, child, tomorrow and tomorrow still,
And every tomorrow hope; trust while you live.
Hope, each time the dawn doth heaven fill,
Be there to ask as God is there to give.*
VICTOR HUGO

*Sad soul, take comfort nor forget
The sunrise never failed us yet.*
CELIA LAIGHTON THAXTER

MEDITATION

The first rays of a sunrise are subtle at best. Slowly the darkness begins to fade as the sun makes its way toward the horizon. Then as the giant orb of fire climbs up into view, the entire sky changes color. Depending on the cloud cover and other atmospheric influences, the sunrise can look different each and every day, but because we can count on it to happen without fail, it's a wonderful symbol for the hope we have in Christ.

It was a dark, bleak day when Jesus died on the cross—the worst day His followers had ever known. And yet, when the grieving women ran to the tomb early in the morning of the third day, after the sun had risen, they were greeted with the glorious news of the resurrection! Praise God we can be sure that those who believe in His Son will also know the glory of everlasting life. We can be even more certain of that than we are of the sunrise. For no matter what darkness our life holds, one day we will be bathed in the light of heaven forever.

Are you placing your hope in that of which you can be sure? Is yours a "sunrise hope" that never disappoints you? If not, it's never too late. The next time you are blessed to watch a sunrise, think about the hope that it represents: the hope of your own resurrection into the light of heaven someday. It's a hope that never fades, and never disappoints.

For Reflection or Discussion

- In what, or in whom, do you place your hope? Is any of your hope ill-founded or misplaced?
- What happens when we place our hope in the wrong things or the wrong people?
- Are you as sure of eternal life as you are of the sunrise? Why or why not?

A Thought to Share

Life with Christ is an endless hope, without Him a hopeless end.

Suggestion for the Week

How long has it been since you've seen the sun rise? If possible, plan a morning this week when you can get up early and sit facing the sunrise. It will fill you with new hope for the day.

Suggested Hymns

- The Solid Rock
- Great Is Thy Faithfulness

Prayer Requests and Closing Prayer

LESSON 42
Making Each Day Count

KEY VERSE

This is the day the Lord has made; let us rejoice and be glad in it.
PSALM 118:24

OPENING PRAYER

LORD, LET US NEVER FORGET the treasure of each day. You present our days to us so clean and new, so full of opportunity. May we always remember that every day is a good day when You are a part of it. In Your precious name we pray, amen.

INTRODUCTION

The older we get the less likely we are to take an ordinary day for granted. Illness and tragedy can come around more often as we age, and so an ordinary day can become a gift to be treasured.

But do we really appreciate the ordinary day? Isn't it our nature to look for something different or exciting to happen? We want to be entertained, surprised, and at least visited for goodness sakes, but on many an ordinary day, none of those things may take place.

What does it take to make each day count—to see the value in the ordinary days that we see in the special ones? Sometimes it takes not being able to experience the ordinary for a while. The ordinary day begins to look good to us when we suffer an illness or injury and can't go about our normal routine. Then we strive to get back to the days of normalcy we enjoyed before.

Often people tend to say, when asked about their day, "It's just a day like any other" or "It's just another day." When we are wise, we recognize that those statements shouldn't be said in a downcast tone. They should be shouted from the rooftops and celebrated! Each day is a gift waiting to be opened—even the ordinary ones.

We can embrace the day whatever it brings when we truly understand that the God who loves us created each day for us—and that nothing that will happen to us within the span of a day will take Him by surprise.

FOR REFLECTION OR DISCUSSION

- Do you think you appreciate the gift of the ordinary day? Why or why not?
- In your opinion, what constitutes a "good" day?
- Name some things we can all do to make each day better for ourselves and others.

SCRIPTURES AND QUOTES

Better is one day in your courts than a thousand elsewhere;
I would rather be a doorkeeper in the house of my God
than dwell in the tents of the wicked.
PSALM 84:10

Teach us to number our days aright, that we may gain a heart of wisdom.
PSALM 90:12

"Give us each day our daily bread."
LUKE 11:3

Though outwardly we are wasting away,
yet inwardly we are being renewed day by day.
2 CORINTHIANS 4:16

But encourage one another daily, as long as it is called Today.
HEBREWS 3:13

Each day presents gifts of its own.
ANONYMOUS

Each day the world is born anew
For him who takes it rightly.
JAMES RUSSELL LOWELL

MEDITATION

The world is full of suggestions as to how we should spend each day. The best advice of all may be to let prayer be the "bookends" on our day—meaning that we begin and end each day with prayer. We might begin each morning asking the Lord to guide us through the day, bringing to mind those things He would have us do. We might ask Him to open our eyes to the blessings, grace and miracles, which are always a part of even the most ordinary day. Once we pray that, we need to let go of our own plans, because God may have something very different in store for us!

Then, at the end of the day, we should remember to thank the Lord for everything that happened, because it was part of the day He gave us. Those who end each day with a grateful heart, and express their gratitude to God in prayer, will have a better night's sleep, and thus, a better day tomorrow.

An older woman proclaimed that she began each day with just a three-word prayer: "Lord, use me." Once she had done that, she went through the day anticipating that the Lord would put someone in her path who needed her attention. Whether she was called to perform a small act of kindness or a more significant one, she was prepared because she went through the day "on assignment" from the Lord!

Every day we live counts in God's kingdom. We can waste our days thinking about the past or worrying about the future, or we can really be present each and every day—full of wonder at what God is going to do in and through us.

FOR REFLECTION OR DISCUSSION

- Is there such a thing as a useless day? Why or why not?
- What can we do to make each day we live count for something?
- How could keeping a "gratitude journal" help us appreciate the days of our lives?

A Thought to Share

We know not what today holds, but we know who holds today.

Suggestion for the Week

Try beginning each day with a simple prayer asking the Lord to use you in some way. Then get ready for a day of adventure with Him!

Suggested Hymns

- This Is the Day
- Better is One Day
- Day by Day

Prayer Requests and Closing Prayer

LESSON 43
Remembering Spiritual Milestones

KEY VERSE

The Lord has done great things for us, and we are filled with joy.
PSALM 126:3

OPENING PRAYER

O LORD, OF ALL THE THINGS we may forget, we don't want to forget all that You have done for us in our lifetimes. And so we ask, with humble hearts, that You would bring to mind those times when You intervened in our lives that we might gain strength for the present day and hope for the future from the works of Your faithful, loving hand. In Your holy name we pray, amen.

INTRODUCTION

Living in the past isn't necessarily a healthy way to spend our remaining days on earth, but sometimes remembering the past can bring new hope and life into the present.

Psychologists sometimes ask people to trace their life story in terms of what the most important events or turning points were. Our lists may include getting a degree, serving in the military, getting married, having children, launching a business, or losing a loved one. All those are key events that took our lives down a certain path and shaped who we would ultimately become.

We have different ways of remembering the milestones in our lives. Often photos mark the occasion, or perhaps we received a gold watch or a special plaque to commemorate a particular achievement. But the events that shaped us often need no reminders. Rather they are a permanent part of who we are.

So it is with the spiritual milestones we have in our life. A call to serve, a commitment to the Lord, a baptism, or a time we were afraid or alone and felt the Lord's presence—all these and more may be in our personal collection of spiritual milestones. When we add our memories of what God has done in our lives—prayers answered, insights offered, comfort provided—we can see that ours is a rich legacy to remember.

For Reflection or Discussion

- What key events in your life contributed most to who you are today?
- How do you remember those milestones?
- In what ways does your past give you strength for today and hope for the future?

Scriptures and Quotes

He [Moses] got up early the next morning and built an altar at the foot of the mountain and set up twelve stone pillars representing the twelve tribes of Israel.
Exodus 24:4

Remember the days of old; consider the generations long past.
Deuteronomy 32:7

"In the future, when your children ask you, 'What do these stones mean?' tell them that the flow of the Jordan was cut off before the ark of the covenant of the Lord. When it crossed the Jordan, the waters of the Jordan were cut off. These stones are to be a memorial to the people of Israel forever."
Joshua 4:6-7

Elijah took twelve stones, one for each of the tribes descended from Jacob,
to whom the word of the Lord had come… With the stones he built an
altar in the name of the Lord, and he dug a trench around it
large enough to hold two seahs of seed.
1 KINGS 18:31-32

Lord, you have been our dwelling place throughout all generations.
PSALM 90:1

We have come to share in Christ if we hold firmly
till the end the confidence we had at first.
HEBREWS 3:14

He who has an ear, let him hear what the Spirit says to the churches.
To him who overcomes, I will give some of the hidden manna.
I will also give him a white stone with a new name written on it,
known only to him who receives it.
REVELATION 2:17

God cares about our remembering Him and what He has done…
God doesn't want us ever to forget what He has done, or who He is…
Reflections on His character give us courage for the future. [56]
CHARLES R. SWINDOLL

MEDITATION

A tour of the Holy Land is punctuated by places where someone erected a memorial of some kind to remember something God did. One is on Mt. Carmel where Elijah called down fire from heaven to send the Baal worshipers running away in fear. A monument marks the spot where the prophet built the altar with the trench around it. In Bethlehem, a magnificent cathedral, the Church of the Nativity, marks the spot where Jewish tradition says Jesus Christ was born in a stable. Another church, poised on a hillside with breathtaking views of the Sea of Galilee, marks the spot where Jesus gave the Sermon on the Mount. Guides assure travelers to Israel that, due to the efficacy of the Jewish oral tradition, these spots are accurate.

Are we as faithful about marking the spiritual milestones in our lives? Can we even recall with certainty the times we are sure the Lord spoke to us, answered our prayers, or intervened to lead us in a better direction? If not, it's not too late to think about these milestones and to share what we remember with our children and grandchildren as part of a lasting legacy.

Teacher and pastor Chuck Swindoll offers three steps to creating a legacy through spiritual milestones: remember, create, and impart. He encourages us to remember the spiritual milestones that we need to commemorate however we must trigger our minds to remember. He also suggests we create physical reminders of what God has done in our lives, whether it's a prayer journal, a collection of favorite Scripture verses, or a photo or object that reminds us of a time when God played an active role. And lastly, he urges us to impart to the next generation what God has done in our lives. "God is deeply concerned that the next generation learns about Him. That happens best through us," Swindoll wrote.[57]

So remember, create, and impart. These three steps pass on the spiritual milestones that have the power to encourage the next generation. Because they are the works of God's hands, milestones also have the power to encourage us for the day ahead. Oh what wondrous things God has done! Let us never forget His mighty works, nor neglect to share them with others.

FOR REFLECTION OR DISCUSSION

- Can you recall a spiritual milestone in your life that is significant to you?
- What have you done, or what could you do, to commemorate that milestone?
- How might you best share a legacy of spiritual milestones with future generations?

A THOUGHT TO SHARE

Life is like an art gallery. On exhibit are all the things God has done for us.

SUGGESTION FOR THE WEEK

Take one memory you have of something God did in your life and recognize it as a spiritual milestone. Create something physical to commemorate what happened, even if all you do is write it down, and share it with someone in a younger generation.

SUGGESTED HYMNS

- How Great Thou Art
- O God, Our Help in Ages Past
- To God Be the Glory

PRAYER REQUESTS AND CLOSING PRAYER

NOTES

LESSON 44
Plugging into the Power

KEY VERSE

You are awesome, O God, in your sanctuary; the God of Israel
gives power and strength to his people. Praise be to God!
PSALM 68:35

OPENING PRAYER

O LORD, TOO OFTEN we get discouraged when we notice
ourselves growing weaker and weaker. Keep us mindful, O Lord,
that we don't have to rely on our own strength alone, for You are all
powerful, and Your power is always available to us. In Your awesome
name we pray, amen.

INTRODUCTION

Why is it that tasks we used to do so easily seem so monumental
when we age? How many thousands of times did we stand up
unassisted out of a chair in our lifetime? Now it may take several tries
if we are able to do it at all!

Getting discouraged about our physical frailties is certainly
understandable and, unfortunately, is often a normal aspect of
growing older. With the blessing of being permitted to live a long life
comes the challenge of living a long life, right? As with most of life,
we must take the good with the bad as we come to understand that
not everything is in our control.

Nutrition and exercise can help to an extent, but eventually we
must come to terms with the fact that there is no fountain of youth,
and we will decline physically the longer we live. The human body is

miraculous in its ability to recover, and modern medicine has made great strides replacing bad joints and transplanting organs. Yet no one has come up with a medication that guarantees we will age without losing any of our former strength. Humans, unlike cell phones, can't simply be plugged into an electrical outlet to be recharged.

But that doesn't mean we are powerless—quite the contrary. Believers of Jesus Christ can plug into the almighty power that is His anytime we want to through prayer. His power becomes our power, and as the favorite old song "Jesus Loves Me" says, "I am weak but He is strong."

For Reflection or Discussion

- What is the most frustrating aspect of growing older for you?
- What activities do you do regularly to stave off the aging process?
- Do you notice yourself growing weaker in the physical sense? What other changes do you notice?

Scriptures and Quotes

Great is our Lord and mighty in power;
His understanding has no limit.
Psalm 147:5

"But you will receive power when the Holy Spirit comes on you;
and you will be my witnesses in Jerusalem, and in all Judea
and Samaria, and to the ends of the earth."
Acts 1:8

I am not ashamed of the gospel, because it is the power of God
for the salvation of everyone who believes.
Romans 1:16

By his power God raised the Lord from the dead,
and he will raise us also.
1 Corinthians 6:14

"My grace is sufficient for you, for my power is made perfect in weakness."
2 CORINTHIANS 12:9

Now to him who is able to do immeasurably more than all we ask or
imagine, according to his power that is at work within us, to him be glory
in the church and in Christ Jesus throughout all generations,
for ever and ever! Amen.
EPHESIANS 3:20

And we pray this in order that you may live a life worthy of the Lord...
being strengthened with all power according to his glorious might
so that you may have great endurance and patience.
COLOSSIANS 1:10, 11

For God did not give us a spirit of timidity,
but a spirit of power, of love and of self-discipline.
2 TIMOTHY 1:7

No pressure is greater than God's power. [58]
CHARLES R. SWINDOLL

Before He furnishes the abundant supply, we must first be
made conscious of our emptiness. Before He gives strength,
we must be made to feel our weakness.[59]
ARTHUR W. PINK

MEDITATION

God tells us that His power is made perfect in weakness. That
being inarguably true, we should be grateful for our weakness, for
God can't fill us with His power until we acknowledge that we need it.

We live in a society that rewards a "can do" attitude, so it is
sometimes difficult for us to say, "Lord, I really can't do this without
You. I need Your strength to see me through." But those are the very
words the Lord wants to hear from us. Once we are empty of our
own power, He can completely fill us up with His almighty power.
Then and only then can we say the words of Philippians 4:13 with
conviction: *I can do everything through him who gives me strength.*

And God will always give us just the amount of strength and power that we need. Sometimes we may ask for the power to move mountains, but other times we may just request the strength to get dressed for the day, or the power to keep a positive attitude when surrounded by negative messages.

So often we go through the day feeling powerless only because we haven't plugged in to the power that God makes available to us—the very same power that raised Christ from the dead! (Romans 8:11; Ephesians 1:18-20) Once we truly believe that God will provide the power we need in any situation, we don't have to feel powerless ever again. We only have to come to Him humbly and ask Him to refill and recharge us, and He will.

The Apostle Paul sent a beautiful benediction to the church in Rome: *May the God of hope fill you with all joy and peace as you trust in him, so that you may overflow with hope by the power of the Holy Spirit* (Romans 15:13). May that same power, which comes from the Lord, be yours in abundance today.

FOR REFLECTION OR DISCUSSION

- Are there times when you feel weak and helpless?
- How can we tap into God's power when we feel powerless?
- How do we know God is powerful? What is His most powerful promise to you?

A THOUGHT TO SHARE

You won't get the power if you don't plug in!

SUGGESTION FOR THE WEEK

Spend some time in prayer asking the Lord to strengthen you by His power in areas of weakness.

Suggested Hymns

- Jesus Loves Me
- There Is Power in the Blood

Prayer Requests and Closing Prayer

NOTES

LESSON 45
What a Friend

KEY VERSE

*"I no longer call you servants, for a servant does not know
his master's business. Instead, I have called you friends, for
everything that I learned from my Father I have made known to you."*
JOHN 15:15

OPENING PRAYER

O LORD, HOW PRIVILEGED WE ARE that You have called us Your
friends. Forgive us for those times when we haven't been the kind of
friends You deserve, Lord: those times when we've been too focused
on ourselves to connect with You. We thank You for the blessing of
friendship with one another, and for the blessed gift of our friendship
with You. In Your precious name we pray, amen.

INTRODUCTION

Of all the gifts the Lord gives us, friendship is one of the best!
A few friends stand out in our memories and our hearts when we
are older and can reflect back over a lifetime. These are the people
whose names and faces we will never forget. Even if they have passed
on before us, we still remember their laugh, their smile, their caring
touch, as if we were with them only yesterday.

That's the kind of friend we want to be to others, isn't it? A
woman who moved into assisted living told her daughters, "I don't
need to make friends with any of these old people here. I've had
enough friends in my life." But of course she did. She played bridge
with the same ladies week after week and they became very close to

one another. When one of them passed away, the woman told her daughters, "I really loved her, you know." We take a chance on being hurt when we take a chance on friendship, but it's a chance worth taking.

Friendship is a bridge between two hearts. True friends can sense when one of them is feeling down without any words being spoken. Even when miles separate them, they often sense when one of them needs the other to get in touch. They are connected deeply.

We make close friendships when we are willing to spend time with another person. The more we get to know them, the more we trust them. The more we trust them, the closer we are to them.

That's how it is with Jesus. He wants to be our friend, and so He asks that we spend time with Him and learn to trust Him. He is a friend who will never disappoint us in any way.

For Reflection or Discussion

- When you hear the word friend, who comes to mind?
- What is the difference between a friend and an acquaintance?
- Are you willing to make new friends in your life now?

Scriptures and Quotes

A friend loves at all times.
Proverbs 17:17

Perfume and incense bring joy to the heart, and the pleasantness of one's friend springs from his earnest counsel.
Proverbs 27:9

*"Greater love has no one than this,
that he lay down his life for his friends."*
John 15:13

"You are my friends if you do what I command."
John 15:14

"This is my command: Love each other."
JOHN 15:17

*"Father, I want those you have given me to be with me where I am,
and to see my glory, the glory you have given me because
you loved me before the creation of the world."*
JOHN 17:24

*And the Scripture was fulfilled that says, "Abraham believed God, and it
was credited to him as righteousness," and he was called God's friend.*
JAMES 2:23

*God evidently does not intend us all to be rich, or powerful or great,
but He does intend us all to be friends.*
RALPH WALDO EMERSON

*A true friend is a gift of God, and He only
who made hearts can unite them.*
ROBERT SOUTH

*When once we get intimate with Jesus we are never lonely, we never need
sympathy, we can pour out all the time without being pathetic.* [60]
OSWALD CHAMBERS

MEDITATION

To be in an intimate relationship with Jesus, we must change our focus from "what kind of friend is Jesus to me?" to "what kind of friend am I to Jesus?" Do we tell Him our joyful secrets as well as our sorrows? Do we praise Him and thank Him as often as we ask things of Him? A friend would do that and more.

We can understand our friendship with Jesus when we think about what makes our earthly friendships significant. Loyalty comes to mind. So does dedication to staying in touch, spending time together when possible. Jesus Christ expects no less of us once we are in an intimate relationship with Him.

Because Jesus is God, He knows our innermost fears and hurts, but He wants us to open up our hearts and share them with Him.

When we do that, we allow Him to shine His light on every situation and that enables us to see our struggles more clearly—to see them as Jesus does.

Like a good friend, Jesus also welcomes us to spend time with Him. Friends don't always have to talk to communicate. Jesus is the kind of friend who is so close, we can be in His presence at all times—and He is there with us even if we don't have the strength or the inclination to say anything at all.

How privileged we are to have a friend in the heavenly realms—one who promises to stand up for us and to welcome us into His presence some day! Just as we go out of our way to encourage and support our earthly friends, we must remember to send praises to Jesus for being the kind of friend who will never let us down. What a friend we have in Jesus!

For Reflection or Discussion

- Do you feel that you have an intimate relationship with Jesus Christ?
- If so, in what ways do you experience His friendship?
- How can your friendship with Jesus be more real to you?

A Thought to Share

Friends are those who see our faults and love us anyway.

Suggestion for the Week

To have a friend, we need to be a friend. Endeavor to make a new friend this week—and eventually, introduce your new friend to your friend Jesus!

Suggested Hymns

- What a Friend We Have in Jesus
- Nearer, My God, To Thee

Prayer Requests and Closing Prayer

LESSON 46

At the Cross

KEY VERSE

He himself bore our sins in his body on the tree, so that we might die to sins and live for righteousness; by his wounds you have been healed.
1 PETER 2:24

OPENING PRAYER

O LORD, MAY WE NEVER take too lightly the sacrifice You made for us when You died upon the cross. We want to keep the image of the cross ever before us, Lord, that we might remember and praise You all the days of our lives. In Your precious name, amen.

INTRODUCTION

Believe it or not, the cross has become something of a fashion statement. Runway models are photographed with large crosses around their necks—crosses made of metal or encrusted with sequins or jewels. How interesting that this symbol, a reminder of God's amazing gift of salvation, has been relegated to a meaningless fashion icon by the unbelieving world. Quite possibly this is another of Satan's pitiful attempts to obscure the true meaning of Christianity.

Of course, the cross in Roman times was as torturous and dreaded as the guillotine was in later generations. (Interesting that people don't wear miniature guillotines around their necks!) Roman roadways would be lined with crosses bearing crucified citizens who failed to honor Caesar or committed some other perceived crime against the Roman Empire. Most were crucified upside down, a gruesome but quicker way to die than the crucifixion of Christ.

The movie *Passion of the Christ* did an excellent job of portraying the horrors of the beating and the agony of the crucifixion of Jesus. Historians tell us that the only way Jesus could take a breath was to push up against His feet to relieve the pressure on His lungs—the same feet that had a nail driven through them.

No, there is nothing beautiful about the physical cross itself, nothing desirable about death by crucifixion. But because of what the cross symbolizes to those who believe in Jesus Christ, it will always be beautiful to us. We will always be drawn to the cross.

FOR REFLECTION OR DISCUSSION

- Have you, or do you, wear a cross necklace? What does it mean to you?
- How can a symbol bring us closer to that which it symbolizes? Can you think of other examples of icons or symbols that do that?
- Why do you think the cross has become popular even with those who don't acknowledge it as a Christian symbol?

SCRIPTURES AND QUOTES

"If anyone would come after me, he must deny himself and take up his cross daily and follow me. For whoever wants to save his life will lose it, but whoever loses his life for me will save it."
LUKE 9:23-24

"And anyone who does not carry his cross and follow me cannot be my disciple."
LUKE 14:27

For the message of the cross is foolishness to those who are perishing, but to us who are being saved it is the power of God.
1 CORINTHIANS 1:18

May I never boast except in the cross of our Lord Jesus Christ, through which the world has been crucified to me, and I to the world.
GALATIANS 6:14

And being found in appearance as a man, he humbled himself and
became obedient to death—even death on a cross!
PHILIPPIANS 2:8

He himself bore our sins in his body on the tree, so that we might die
to sins and live for righteousness; by his wounds you have been healed.
1 PETER 2:24

The cross of Christ is the sweetest burden that I ever bore;
it is such a burden as wings are to a bird, or sails to a ship,
to carry me forward to my harbor.
SAMUEL RUTHERFORD

No cross, no crown.
ENGLISH PROVERB

The Cross was a superb triumph in which the foundations of hell
were shaken. There is nothing more certain in time or eternity
than what Jesus Christ did on the Cross: He switched the whole
of the human race back into a right relationship with God. [61]
OSWALD CHAMBERS

Carry the cross patiently, and with perfect submission;
and in the end it shall carry you.
THOMAS Á KEMPIS

MEDITATION

A popular illustration used by those who explain the gospel message to others has God on one side of a deep chasm and man on the other side. When the cross is laid across the chasm, then man has a route to God. This simple illustration is full of profound truth.

A pastor wanted to create a lasting impression on his congregation about this same truth. One Sunday he stood in front of the church with a roll of tickets, similar to the ones you might get for admittance to a carnival ride back in the old days. As he talked about all the things people mistakenly think might gain them entry into heaven—being a good person, giving money to the poor, attending church regularly, etc.—he rolled more tickets off the roll onto the floor. Soon all the tickets were on the floor forming a huge pile, and he made the point that even all those tickets won't get us admission to heaven without our acceptance of the sacrifice Jesus made for us on the cross!

However you tell the story, it is the basis of our Christian belief. Without the cross, we have no hope. Without the cross, life comes to a meaningless end. But with the cross and God's gift of salvation, all heaven is open to us for eternity!

It's always good to remember that crucifixion was not something done to Jesus. It was something He chose for our sakes. The crowds who shouted, "Crucify him!" didn't know they were actually fulfilling the plan God had designed for closing the gap between Himself and sinful man since before time began.

How sobering it is for each one of us to think that even if we were the only person on earth, Jesus would still go to the cross for us! That's how complete His love for us is. His sacrifice on the cross guarantees those who believe in Him that we will join Him in heaven for all eternity. We must be ever grateful for the cross.

For Reflection or Discussion

- Have you thought about Christ's agony on the cross?
- How can we thank Christ for the sacrifice He made for us?
- What feelings emerge as you gaze upon the cross?

A Thought to Share

The ground at the foot of the cross is level. Everyone is welcome there.

Suggestion for the Week

It's been said that every bird that flies carries the shape of the cross heavenward! Where else in your environment can you discover the shape of the cross? Wherever you see it this week, be blessed by what it represents.

Suggested Hymns

- The Old Rugged Cross
- Beneath the Cross of Jesus
- When I Survey the Wondrous Cross

Prayer Requests and Closing Prayer

NOTES

LESSON 47
His Will, Not Ours

KEY VERSE

Teach me to do your will, for you are my God;
may your good Spirit lead me on level ground.
PSALM 143:10

OPENING PRAYER

O LORD, HOW OFTEN WE GET IN THE WAY of what You are doing in our world! Keep us ever mindful of your plans, Lord God, so we can assist You, not hinder You. In Your precious name we pray, amen.

INTRODUCTION

The ongoing battle of the Christian life is to surrender our will to God's will. Just when we think we've learned the lesson in one aspect of our lives, we discover another area where we are desperately trying to control people, situations, or outcomes. We are frustratingly human and almost incurable in that regard. We want to be in control.

It is perhaps in parenting that we get our strongest lessons in letting go and letting God have control. A single mom cried herself to sleep every night over her rebellious teenage son whom she loved so much. One night, the Lord spoke to her as if in a dream and said, "If you do not let go of that boy, I can't do anything with him." The next morning she knew that she had to abandon all her efforts to "fix" her son. She had to turn him over to God. The ensuing events weren't the ones she would have planned, but God used failure and desperation to turn her son around and make him an awesome man of God. She couldn't have accomplished the same thing no matter how hard she tried.

Many people never come to God because they can't imagine themselves not being in control of their own fate. They have embraced the whole humanistic belief system that tells them they are in control of their lives—the captains of their ships, the masters of their fate. They can't imagine handing that complete control over to God.

And yet, the truth is that they aren't really in control at all! Often it takes a devastating tragedy, a failed marriage, or a serious illness for people to realize that they simply aren't in charge—God is! God doesn't promise to spare us from trouble but promises to be with us through it. He is all powerful and can use any adverse situation to our benefit and to His glory—if we will allow Him to do so.

For Reflection or Discussion

- Was there anything in your life that you struggled to control, only to find out in the end that you were unable to do so?
- Why do you think so many of us are afraid to relinquish control?
- How can giving up control mean gaining freedom?

Scriptures and Quotes

"Our Father in heaven, hallowed be your name, your kingdom come, your will be done on earth as it is in heaven."
Matthew 6:9-10

"Are not two sparrows sold for a penny? Yet not one of them will fall to the ground apart from the will of your Father. And even the very hairs of your head are all numbered. So don't be afraid; you are worth more than many sparrows."
Matthew 10:29-31

Going a little farther, he fell with his face to the ground and prayed, "My Father, if it is possible, may this cup be taken from me. Yet not as I will, but as you will."
Matthew 26:39

"For I have come down from heaven not to do my will but to do the will of him who sent me. And this is the will of him who sent me, that I shall lose none of all that he has given me, but raise them up on the last day. For my Father's will is that everyone who looks to the Son and believes in him shall have eternal life, and I will raise him up at the last day."
JOHN 6:38-40

Do not conform any longer to the pattern of this world, but be transformed by the renewing of your mind. Then you will be able to test and approve what God's will is—his good, pleasing and perfect will.
ROMANS 12:2

Therefore do not be foolish, but understand what the Lord's will is.
EPHESIANS 5:17

It is God who works in you to will and to act according to his good purpose.
PHILIPPIANS 2:13

This is the confidence we have in approaching God: that if we ask anything according to his will, he hears us.
1 JOHN 5:14

The only important decision we have to make is to live with God; He will make the rest.
ANONYMOUS

We are all dangerous folk without God's controlling hand.
WILLIAM WARD AYER

MEDITATION

Jesus, who was divine, submitted to the will of the Father. We haven't given this truth the place it deserves in our hearts if that realization doesn't move us. Because He was also human, the Son of Man, Jesus prayed in Gethsemane for the cup to pass Him by, and yet He also prayed, *"nevertheless not as I will, but as thou wilt"* (Matthew 26:39, KJV).

Jesus knew it was only in fulfilling the Father's will that His life on earth would fulfill its purpose. The same is true for us. Plan as we might, our plans will not succeed completely unless they are also God's plans for us. When we find out what God is doing and join Him in it, then we also know His will for our lives. We are blessed when we walk in it.

How do we know His will? First, we have to silence any schemes or dreams that are ours and ours alone. We have to lay them before the Father and ask Him for His blessing or His clear message that this direction is not for us. Each day we must ask Him to make His will known to us so that our time is spent in fulfillment of His plans, not our own. He can and will open and shut doors when we relinquish control to Him. We just have to let go!

Once we are living in the will of God for our lives, it's as if we have the wind at our back. That wind is most likely the Holy Spirit. We may be going in the wrong direction if most of life feels like we are walking into the wind. Yet it's never too late to lay it all down again: to simply ask the Lord to show us His will for our lives each day, and to walk in it.

And so we say with the writer of Hebrews: *May the God of peace, who through the blood of the eternal covenant brought back from the dead our Lord Jesus, that great Shepherd of the sheep, equip you with everything good for doing his will, and may he work in us what is pleasing to him, through Jesus Christ, to whom be glory for ever and ever. Amen* (Hebrews 13:20-21).

For Reflection or Discussion

- When you think about your life now, do you feel like the wind is at your back or in your face? Why do you think you feel the way you do?
- In what ways has God revealed to you His purpose for your life?
- How can you walk in His purpose for you the rest of your days on earth?

A Thought to Share

If God is your co-pilot, switch seats!

Suggestion for the Week

Think of one area of your life that you are holding tightly, trying to control it. Release it to God and ask that His will be done, not yours.

Suggested Hymns

- Be Thou My Vision
- Take My Life and Let it Be
- Have Thine Own Way, Lord

Prayer Requests and Closing Prayer

NOTES

LESSON 48

Blessed Assurance

KEY VERSE

Let us draw near to God with a sincere heart in full assurance of faith.
HEBREWS 10:22

OPENING PRAYER

O LORD, WE KNOW that You are the one person we can trust completely. Don't allow doubts to seep in and rob us of the faith we have in You and in Your promises, Lord. We pray that You would keep our faith strong, a testimony to the blessed assurance that is ours. In Your precious name we pray, amen.

INTRODUCTION

Oh the many things we do to try to be more secure. We lock our doors. We purchase fire extinguishers. We carry mace in our purses. We wear automated call buttons around our necks in case we fall and can't get up! All those things may be wise, but they aren't where our real security lies, are they?

Those whose business it is to sell us these products, along with insurance salesmen and alarm companies, tend to use scare tactics to get us to purchase their products. Now the big scare is identity theft. We are told to shred our important papers, never put outgoing checks in our personal mailboxes, and to purchase identity theft insurance. Identity theft is horrible if it happens to you, but what are the odds that it will? And can paying a monthly fee really deter a determined thief?

The truth is, we are sometimes wise to take security precautions and certainly the proper form of insurance can bring peace of mind to us and to our loved ones. But not even Snoopy and MetLife, or the good hands people at Allstate, can guarantee us eternal life, can they? We try to keep the wolf from the door and ourselves and everyone we love safe at all times, but we live in a fallen world and so bad things sometimes happen in spite of all our efforts.

Our real security is found only in trusting in Jesus Christ as our Lord and Savior. Then we have the blessed assurance of eternal life.

For Reflection or Discussion

- What security steps have you taken the last few years? Why?
- Do you feel safe on a daily basis? Why or why not?
- Why do you think security measures and insurance give us peace of mind? Is it true peace of mind?

Scriptures and Quotes

The eternal God is your refuge, and underneath are the everlasting arms.
DEUTERONOMY 33:27

"For God so loved the world that he gave his one and only Son, that whoever believes in him shall not perish but have eternal life."
JOHN 3:16

"My sheep listen to my voice; I know them, and they follow me, I give them eternal life, and they shall never perish; no one can snatch them out of my hand."
JOHN 10:27-28

Therefore, there is now no condemnation for those who are in Christ Jesus, because through Christ Jesus the law of the Spirit of life set me free from the law of sin and death.
ROMANS 8:1-2

For I am convinced that neither death nor life, neither angels nor demons,
neither the present nor the future, nor any powers, neither height nor
depth, nor anything else in all creation, will be able to separate us from
the love of God that is in Christ Jesus our Lord.
ROMANS 8:38-39

I know whom I have believed, and am convinced that he is able
to guard what I have entrusted to him for that day.
2 TIMOTHY 1:12

Let us hold unswervingly to the hope we profess,
for he who promised is faithful.
HEBREWS 10:23

Praise be to the God and Father of our Lord Jesus Christ! In his
great mercy he has given us new birth into a living hope through the
resurrection of Jesus Christ from the dead, and into an inheritance that
can never perish, spoil or fade—kept in heaven for you...
1 PETER 1:3

Why didn't someone tell me that I can become a Christian
and settle the doubts afterward?
WILLIAM RAINEY HARPER

Beware of despairing about yourself. You are commanded
to put your trust in God, and not in yourself.
ST. AUGUSTINE

MEDITATION

Our real security is not in anything we can purchase or achieve
for ourselves. Our real security is in Jesus Christ because of who He
is and His promises to us. The Bible is full of the promises of God to
His people, and not one is a false or exaggerated promise. The one
thing of which we can always be sure is that God will do what He says
He will do. If He says we will have eternal life if we accept His Son
as Lord and Savior, then we will have eternal life. That is our blessed
assurance.

Many people have been led closer to an understanding of how secure and complete God's love for them is by the words to the hymn "Blessed Assurance," which Fanny J. Crosby wrote in 1873. She was blind from the age of six weeks due to poor medical care, yet she wrote more than 8,000 gospel song texts in her lifetime of almost 95 years. She passed away in 1915, and engraved on her tombstone in Bridgeport, Connecticut, are the words Jesus spoke of the woman who anointed His head with oil, *"She did what she could"* (Mark 14:8).

The songs we sing, the Bible verses we read or commit to memory, the ways we see God working in our life and the lives of those around us do more to give us a sense of security than the strongest deadbolt lock we could purchase. In his book *A Long Obedience in the Same Direction*, Eugene Peterson wrote, "All the persons of faith I know are sinners, doubters, uneven performers. We are secure not because we are sure of ourselves, but because we trust that God is sure of us." [62]

Our true security, our blessed assurance, is not based on feelings or even on facts. It is based on faith—a faith that we can count on in every circumstance.

For Reflection or Discussion

- Would you say you spend most of your time anxious, or at peace?
- How can trusting in the blessed assurance God gives us also make us feel more secure on a daily basis?
- What is your greatest fear? Is your faith greater?

A Thought to Share

We're in good hands only when we are in God's hands.

Suggestion for the Week

Review your insurance policies and security measures. Are they adequate and up to date? Now set them aside and meditate on the true Source of your security.

Suggested Hymns

- Blessed Assurance
- I Am Thine, O Lord
- He's Got the Whole World in His Hands

Prayer Requests and Closing Prayer

NOTES

LESSON 49
Be Still and Know

KEY VERSE

"Be still, and know that I am God."
PSALM 46:10

OPENING PRAYER

LORD, IT'S SO EASY FOR US to want to fill our days with noise and activity, even if we know we are pursuing meaningless ways to fill up the voids in our lives. Be patient with us, Lord, as we learn to be content in Your company, for You are all we need—now and forever. In Your name we pray, amen.

INTRODUCTION

We are raising a generation in this country that needs constant noise and entertainment to feel okay about themselves. It began with teenagers saying they couldn't do their homework without listening to music at the same time. It's escalated to the point where many of them may be listening to music, texting, watching TV and studying concurrently.

Now movie theaters must crack down on people making calls or texting on their cell phones during the movie—and many of these offenders are adults. Evidently just watching a film isn't entertaining enough in this digital age.

Yet we need to stop and ask ourselves as a society: What are we trying to escape? Why are we so uncomfortable with silence? Why will we let just any kind of television drivel invade our homes? All we have to do to restore peace and quiet, and maybe have an opportunity to hear ourselves think for the first time all day, is to click the 'off' button on the remote control. As a society, we have become addicted to the din.

But there is another way to live, a way that accepts the gift that quietness brings. Even those of us who feel we have too much quiet in our lives can begin to appreciate the quiet for what it offers us. For it is only when we are still and quiet that we can hear the still, small voice of God in our souls. We do not want to miss His messages, do we?

FOR REFLECTION OR DISCUSSION

- Do you have too much or too little noise and activity in your life right now? Why do you think you feel the way you do?
- What do you do to fill up the silence if it becomes unbearable?
- Are there times when you appreciate being still and quiet?

SCRIPTURES AND QUOTES

The Lord said, "Go out and stand on the mountain in the presence of the Lord, for the Lord is about to pass by." Then a great and powerful wind tore the mountains apart and shattered the rocks before the Lord, but the Lord was not in the wind. After the wind there was an earthquake, but the Lord was not in the earthquake. After the earthquake came a fire, but the Lord was not in the fire. And after the fire came a gentle whisper. When Elijah heard it, he pulled his cloak over his face and went out and stood at the mouth of the cave. Then a voice said to him, "What are you doing here, Elijah?"
1 KINGS 19:11-13

Be still before the Lord and wait patiently for him.
PSALM 37:7

"In repentance and rest is your salvation, in quietness and trust is your strength."
ISAIAH 30:15

"But the Lord is in his holy temple; let all the earth be silent before him."
HABAKKUK 2:20

"Be still before the Lord, all mankind,
because he has roused himself from his holy dwelling."
ZECHARIAH 2:13

Let me not be afraid of silence, for in it I can find you.
NANCY PARKER BRUMMETT

You may not see or feel the inner workings of His silent power,
but rest assured it is always mightily at work. And it will work for you,
if you will only quiet your spirit enough to be carried along
by the current of its power. [63]
HANNAH WHITALL SMITH

Withdraw yourself from all needless distraction, close your ears
to the voices of the world, and be as a docile learner, ever listening
for the heavenly wisdom the Master has to teach.[64]
ANDREW MURRAY

MEDITATION

If we can be perfectly still to have a photograph or x-ray taken, why can't we be still before God? It may be because we think that if we aren't doing something, we are wasting time. However, if we are consciously making an effort to be still before God, we are doing something, aren't we? We are making ourselves available to Him, and He will be pleased to keep us company.

When we are physically ill to the point of weakness, we don't do anything at all. Rather we rest until we are better. Similarly, when we find ourselves spiritually distressed, the best remedy is to be still—to rest in God's presence and allow His healing comfort to embrace us.

A wonderful Hebrew word found throughout the Psalms is the word *Selah*. While there is some debate among scholars as to its exact meaning, many believe it means to pause, stop and listen, or measure carefully. We know that most of the psalms were sung accompanied by musical instruments, so it may also indicate a musical interlude.

But whenever it appears in Scripture that's a good reminder to pause to think about what we have just read. So much instruction, insight, and encouragement is ours to claim if we are only still long enough to receive it. Psalm 4:4 reads: *When you are on your beds, search your hearts and be silent. Selah.* That is an instruction worth following, isn't it? Selah.

For Reflection or Discussion

- When was the last time you were still before God?
- Has God ever communicated with you through times of quiet and stillness?
- How can we create more quiet times with God in our lives now?

A Thought to Share

God's voice can only be heard in the silence of the soul.

Suggestion for the Week

The next time you find yourself sitting perfectly still and quiet, close your eyes and thank God for that solitude—then let Him join you in it.

Suggested Hymns

- Be Still, My Soul
- Be Still and Know
- Take Time to be Holy

Prayer Requests and Closing Prayer

LESSON 50
God's Mysterious Ways

KEY VERSE

"For my thoughts are not your thoughts, neither are your ways my ways," declares the Lord.
ISAIAH 55:8

OPENING PRAYER

LORD, EVEN WHEN WE DON'T UNDERSTAND what You are doing, we still trust You. Help us to accept that, whatever the situation, Your way is always better than any way we might contrive. Help us to rest in the knowledge that Your ways are always best. In Your all-powerful name we pray, amen.

INTRODUCTION

The longer we live the more tragedies and unexplainable events we know about. A man is injured in a bicycle accident six weeks after he is married and he becomes a paraplegic. Weeks later, on the way to sign the lease on a handicap-accessible apartment, his wife is in a head-on collision and is severely injured. She requires back surgery and has a long convalescence. When things like this happen, those who are affected by it, or know the people who are, tend to question who is running the universe.

Earthquakes, tsunamis, tornados, floods—all manner of natural disasters besiege us. Even those who believe God is in control struggle to understand why He allows such pain and devastation in our world. Why would a loving God allow children to be abused, or to starve to death? Why are some people healed while others die? Why are some of our prayers answered while others seem to be ignored?

Because we are human, we will ask these and other questions as long as we live. The absence of concrete answers to these hard questions keeps many people from believing in God. They want a God who is predictable and consistent—if they want a God at all.

It's human to question, but for those who trust God the answer to all the questions life raises is pretty much the same: because God is God and we aren't. God hears and answers all our prayers, but His answer may not be yes or no, but not yet. We won't always understand why He allows the things He allows, but we can always trust that His ways are better than ours.

FOR REFLECTION OR DISCUSSION

- Was there a time in your life when you questioned what God was doing?
- Have you ever pleaded with God for an answer you never got? How did you handle the silence?
- Why do you think bad things happen to good people?

SCRIPTURES AND QUOTES

"We do not know what to do, but our eyes are upon you."
2 CHRONICLES 20:12

Then the Lord answered Job out of the storm. He said: "Who is this that darkens my counsel with words without knowledge?... Where were you when I laid the earth's foundation? Tell me if you understand."
JOB 38:1-2, 4

"For I know the plans I have for you," declares the Lord, "plans to prosper you and not to harm you, plans to give you hope and a future."
JEREMIAH 29:11

And they were in the way going up to Jerusalem; and Jesus went before them: and they were amazed; and as they followed, they were afraid.
MARK 10:32 (KJV)

Now to the King eternal, immortal, invisible, the only God,
be honor and glory for ever and ever. Amen.
1 TIMOTHY 1:17

God moves in a mysterious way
His wonders to perform;
He plants His footsteps in the sea
And rides upon the storm.
WILLIAM COWPER

God is not in the slightest degree baffled or bewildered
by what baffles and bewilders us. [65]
J. B. PHILLIPS

There are three things that only God knows: the beginning of things,
the cause of things, and the end of things.
WELSH PROVERB

MEDITATION

A regular feature of *Guideposts Magazine*, founded by Norman Vincent Peale, is titled "His Mysterious Ways." In each issue, this short, one-page article recounts something miraculous God has done in someone's life. Perhaps a car breaks down and later the disgruntled passenger discovers his or her life was saved because of the disruption. A wedding ring that is lost for years turns up in the garden to comfort a grieving widow. A woman feeling alone in a new city goes to a garage sale and finds her grandmother's dishes—many states removed from where they had been sold. The stories are as varied as the miracles they portray, and the magazine describes this section as ordinary people sharing their "first-hand, chill-down-the-spine experience of God's hidden hand in their lives." No wonder it's the first thing readers turn to when they receive each new issue!

We love to share the stories of how God has worked miraculously in our lives or the lives of others because it helps us get through those times when we really don't understand what God is doing or why. When we believe in a sovereign God, we can never say, "Yes, that bad thing happened, but God didn't have anything to do with it." He is all powerful, all wise, and almighty. He had something to do with it, all right. We just may not know what—or why He allowed it to happen the way it did.

What we must understand is that bad things happen on this earth because of the flesh, the world, or the devil. The flesh isn't meant to last forever, and so illness occurs. The world is fraught with natural and manmade disasters, and the devil prowls around appealing to the sinful nature in all of us. God allows the people He created and loves to have free will. Some make bad choices, and bad things happen.

But praise God, we also know that He can redeem every situation. He can use anything that happens for the good of those who trust and believe in Him. When this earthly life is over, He ensures we are safe with Him forever. We may not always understand His mysterious ways, but we should always trust that His ways are better than ours—and be grateful God is in charge, not us!

For Reflection or Discussion

- Why is it difficult for us to trust when we don't understand?
- When you get to heaven, what's the first question you want to ask God?
- Have you ever struggled with what God was doing only to discover later that He was right and you were wrong?

A Thought to Share

When it's hard to understand God's plan, trust His heart.

Suggestion for the Week

Sometimes it isn't until we are on the other side of a situation that we see how God's hand was at work in the midst of it. Look back over your life for signs of God's mysterious ways at work.

Suggested Hymns

- His Way with Thee
- His Way
- Immortal, Invisible

Prayer Requests and Closing Prayer

NOTES

LESSON 51
Invitation to Glory

KEY VERSE

Christ in you, the hope of glory.
COLOSSIANS 1:27

OPENING PRAYER

O LORD, THAT WHICH WE CAN NEVER DO for ourselves You invite us to do through You. Be with us today, Lord. May the message of salvation through faith alone resonate loudly and clearly in our midst, and may You draw us all closer to You. In Your precious name we pray, amen.

INTRODUCTION

We live in a time, and in a culture, where self-sufficiency is not only valued, it's almost a god to some. Younger people in the height of their careers may position themselves aggressively hoping for the next promotion so they can buy the bigger house, the more expensive car, the designer clothes, or the vacation designed to impress those they know. In times of economic distress, they assume they only have to work harder and smarter—but they never dare to suggest they might lose faith in themselves. The "I can do it" message is deeply ingrained, and for many people, the fear of failure is constant. It's all about being in control.

But the longer we live, the more likely we are to come up against situations, events and relationships that are out of our control. No amount of trying or networking will make a negative lab report turn positive, will it? Jobs are lost through no fault of the employee, and incomes we grow to rely on can dry up in an instant. There is no security based on human effort alone. Eventually all will be lost, and what's left of a life lived successfully becomes nothing more than fodder for a yard sale.

That's a dismal picture, isn't it? It sounds as if all our efforts are worth no more, and leave no more lasting effect, than those of the common ant. And yet that isn't the end of the story of a life lived with an abiding faith in Jesus Christ. Oh, no! The life story of the believer ends on a definite high—the unfailing hope of eternal glory.

FOR REFLECTION OR DISCUSSION

- Was there a time in your life when you thought you had everything under control?
- What happened to make you realize you couldn't control everything?
- Why do you think people in general are so afraid of losing control?

SCRIPTURES AND QUOTES

> *Jesus answered, "I am the way and the truth and the life.*
> *No one comes to the Father except through me."*
> JOHN 14:6

> *For all have sinned and fall short of the glory of God, and are justified freely by his grace through the redemption that came by Christ Jesus.*
> ROMANS 3:23-24

> *For the wages of sin is death, but the gift of God is*
> *eternal life in Christ Jesus our Lord.*
> ROMANS 6:23

> *For it is by grace you have been saved, through faith—and this not from yourselves, it is the gift of God—not by works, so that no one can boast.*
> EPHESIANS 2:8-9

Since, then, you have been raised with Christ, set your hearts on things above, where Christ is seated at the right hand of God... When Christ, who is your life, appears, then you also will appear with him in glory.
COLOSSIANS 3:1, 4

The Lord will rescue me from every evil attack and will bring me safely to his heavenly kingdom. To him be glory for ever and ever. Amen.
2 TIMOTHY 4:18

If God were not willing to forgive sin Heaven would be empty.
GERMAN PROVERB

When by His grace I shall look on His face,
That will be glory, be glory for me. [66]
CHARLES H. GABRIEL

Savior, Savior, Hear my humble cry!
While on others Thou art calling,
Do not pass me by. [67]
FANNY J. CROSBY

If I ever reach heaven I expect to find three wonders there: first, to meet some I had not thought to see there; second, to miss some I had expected to see there; and third, the greatest wonder of all, to find myself there.
JOHN NEWTON

MEDITATION

We often refer to God's gift of salvation as His invitation. Unfortunately, it's an invitation many refuse to accept. They leave it unopened, and because they do not accept it, they will never know the eternal glory God wants to give to them.

But the invitation is still open to those who are willing to receive it! It's an invitation to the most amazing gathering possible: a gathering of the saints, all those who believe, in heaven. Those who accept God's invitation will die to this world, but will live eternally in glory in the company of Jesus Christ. They will join with other believers and will have no suffering, no tears, and no pain.

The steps to salvation, the acceptance of God's invitation to eternal glory, are so simple that many high achievers have difficulty believing that's really all that's necessary. They struggle to believe that they don't have to *do* anything to earn salvation, that it is a gift.

The first step toward salvation is to accept that we are sinners in need of a Savior—and we are all sinners. The second is to accept that God sent Jesus Christ, His Son, to die for our sins to close the gap between us and Him. Next we must truly repent of our sins, and offer an invitation of our own—inviting Jesus to be Lord of our lives. Once we truly believe, we immediately notice a change. All the striving and pain begins to fall away as the Holy Spirit indwells us and encourages us to follow the path of salvation.

Don't refuse God's invitation. It's the most important one you will ever receive, and it guarantees admittance to eternal glory with Him.

For Reflection or Discussion

- Have you accepted God's invitation to eternal life with Him?
- If you have not, why do you think you are still hesitant?
- If you have, share how you came to invite Christ to be your Lord and Savior.

A Thought to Share

There's a train bound for glory! Be on it.

Suggestion for the Week

Do you know someone who still has not accepted God's invitation to glory? Simply tell them what Jesus has done for you, and that He will welcome them, too. If they are willing, lead them in a simple prayer like this: *Lord Jesus, I know that I am a sinner in need of a Savior. I believe that you are the Son of God. Forgive me, Lord, for all my past sins. Please come into my heart now to be the Lord and Savior of my life forever. Amen.* If you haven't taken this step yourself, now's the time!

Suggested Hymns

- Amazing Grace
- Just As I Am
- I'll Fly Away

Prayer Requests and Closing Prayer

NOTES

LESSON 52

Finding Rest in Jesus

KEY VERSE

"Come to me, all you who are weary and burdened,
and I will give you rest."
MATTHEW 11:28

OPENING PRAYER

O LORD, WE TURN to so many different sources for rest and comfort, when all we really need to do is rest in You and in the confidence of Your love for us. Thank You, Lord, for always being our safe place, our place of true rest. In Your name we pray, amen.

INTRODUCTION

"I'm so tired," we may say. Often we are tired because the activities of the day have worn us out, or because we haven't slept well the night before. We can be tired from a lifetime of multi-tasking activity, or just tired because of lack of motivation. Regardless of the cause, we've all had the experience of being weary—and maybe even too tired to sleep.

People go to great extents to get rest when they are tired. Sleep aides may help for a bit. Even sleep clinics have sprung up across the country to monitor sleep patterns of restless patients and advise them on habits or conditions they might change in order to get more sleep. Fitness experts weigh in on the subject and advise that it's not less activity we need when we are tired, but more! A brisk walk around the block to get the blood moving may mean we sleep better at night, and so we try that, too.

And yet the deepest weariness, weariness of the soul, is not so easily fixed. We live in a fallen world, and over the period of a lifetime, many different events and circumstances can "knock the stuffing out of us" as the old expression goes. It's possible to come to the later seasons of our lives not just tired, but bone tired, right down to our marrow. We desperately need rest, and yet as believers in Jesus Christ we know that there is no true rest outside of resting in Jesus.

For Reflection or Discussion

- Do you feel well rested when you wake up in the morning? Why or why not?
- If you are weary, do you see it as a permanent condition here on earth?
- What sorts of things do you do in order to get the rest you need?

Scriptures and Quotes

> *He makes me lie down in green pastures,*
> *he leads me beside quiet waters, he restores my soul.*
> Psalm 23:2-3

> *He who dwells in the shelter of the Most High will rest in the*
> *shadow of the Almighty...He will cover you with his feathers,*
> *and under his wings you will find refuge.*
> Psalm 91:1, 4

> *Be at rest once more, O my soul, for the Lord has been good to you.*
> Psalm 116:7

> *"Stand at the crossroads and look: ask for the ancient paths,*
> *ask where the good way is, and walk in it, and you will*
> *find rest for your souls."*
> Jeremiah 6:16

*"Abide in me, and I in you. As the branch cannot bear fruit of itself,
except it abide in the vine; no more can ye, except ye abide in me."*
JOHN 15:4 (KJV)

*There remains, then, a Sabbath-rest for the people of God; for anyone who
enters God's rest also rests from his own work, just as God did from his.*
HEBREWS 4:9

There is a place of quiet rest near to the heart of God. [68]
CLELAND B. MCAFEE

*Jesus, I am resting, resting
In the joy of what Thou art;
I am finding out the greatness
Of Thy loving heart.* [69]
JEAN S. PIGOTT

*The grace to come and the grace to abide
are alike from Him alone.* [70]
ANDREW MURRAY

*On my part, abiding is nothing but the acceptance of my position, the
consent to be kept there, the surrender of faith to the strong Vine still to
hold the feeble branch. Yes, I will, I do abide in Thee, blessed Lord Jesus.*[71]
ANDREW MURRAY

MEDITATION

A little rabbit once lived in an overgrown juniper bush at the end
of a suburban driveway. Each day the gray bunny ventured out of the
bush to enjoy the sun or nibble on the green grass, but if a storm blew
in, or the neighbor's dog came running by, the little rabbit scurried
back into the bush. She felt safe in the bush and so that's where she
wanted to abide.

It is when we truly abide in Christ that we find rest for our souls,
isn't it?

Andrew Murray, in his classic book *Abide in Christ*, points
out that during His time on earth Jesus most often instructed His

disciples to *follow* Him. "When about to leave for heaven," Murray writes, "He gave them a new word, in which their more intimate and spiritual union with Himself in glory should be expressed." [72] That new word was *abide*.

And so it is with us on our Christian walk. Before we can abide in Jesus, and find true rest for our souls, we must first believe in Him and accept His gift of salvation for us. We must follow Him before we can abide and rest in Him. The more closely we follow Him, the more rest we will have. We will find true rest for our souls when we trust His Word, obey His commandments, and order our lives in such a way that we seek out His company and develop an intimate relationship with Him.

For Reflection or Discussion

- What are some of the safe places we abide in a physical sense?
- Do you have a place to abide when you know you need rest?
- What stops you from finding true rest in Jesus?

A Thought to Share

There's not a specific schedule for resting in Jesus.
His rest is available all day and all night.

Suggestion for the Week

Ask the Lord to be your safe place to abide, and to give you the rest you need. Pay attention to when you feel the most rested. Is it when you have spent time abiding with Him?

Suggested Hymns

- Near to the Heart of God
- Jesus, I Am Resting, Resting
- My Faith Has Found a Resting Place

Prayer Requests and Closing Prayer

Special Holiday Lessons

LESSON 53
Attitude of Gratitude

KEY VERSE

Give thanks in all circumstances, for this is
God's will for you in Christ Jesus.
1 THESSALONIANS 5:18

OPENING PRAYER

LORD, IT'S EASY FOR US TO THANK YOU when things are going well, but You say we are to be thankful in every circumstance. That's harder for us, Lord, and so we come to You with open hearts, asking You to fill us with an attitude of gratitude not just in this season of Thanksgiving, but always. In Your name we pray, amen.

INTRODUCTION

How we cherish the Thanksgiving celebration with all its warm traditions, sights, smells and tastes. More than any other holiday, Thanksgiving is mostly about families and friends gathering together to focus on the blessings they have received, and we appreciate it for its wholesome simplicity.

Of course, while we traditionally think about giving thanks at Thanksgiving, we really need to be grateful to God for all the blessings He has put into our lives every waking moment, not just on special occasions. The older we get, the more we realize that we need to thank God not just for all we have, but also for all we have NOT! If there is a disease we don't have or a family struggle that has passed our family by, that's reason enough to give thanks—and to do so wholeheartedly!

It's amazing how it really is possible to find something for which to be thankful in every situation when you look hard enough. After a traffic accident, are we angry about the crumpled fender, or grateful our head is still in place?

When the weather is bad, do we grumble about not being able to go out or thank God for shelter from the elements? It's all a matter of having the right attitude.

A wonderful faith builder is remembering all the Lord has done for us. It helps us keep everything in our lives in the proper perspective. As we praise Him for the past, we also build hope for the future, and an attitude of gratitude comes more easily to us.

For Reflection or Discussion

- Name some things for which you are grateful today. Remember to include some "everyday delights," small things that bring you happiness.
- Now name some things you are grateful you don't have.
- What keeps us from having an attitude of gratitude as we go through each day?

Scriptures and Quotes

I will remember the deeds of the Lord;
yes, I will remember your miracles of long ago.
Psalm 77:11

Enter his gates with thanksgiving and his courts with praise; give thanks to him and praise his name. For the Lord is good and his love endures forever; his faithfulness continues through all generations.
Psalm 100:4-5

Give thanks to the Lord, for he is good.
Psalm 136:1

Thanks be to God for his indescribable gift!
2 Corinthians 9:15

A grateful thought toward heaven is of itself a prayer. [73]
Gotthold Ephraim Lessing

When we remember, we change how we live our lives.
We change our prayers. Our courage is increased,
our faith is renewed, and we fall more deeply in love with Jesus.[74]
Kelly Hall

Your praise and thanksgiving can help form a highway—a smooth, level
road—on which the Lord can ride forth
unhindered to deliver and bless. [75]
Ruth Myers

Meditation

Even the Lord Jesus gave thanks. When He fed the five thousand with just five loaves and two small fish, we're told He *took the loaves, gave thanks, and distributed to those who were seated as much as they wanted. He did the same with the fish.* (John 6:11). At the Last Supper with His disciples, He *took bread, gave thanks and broke it, and gave it to them* (Luke 22:19). We know that we honor Him when we have gratitude in our hearts, for He is most at home in a grateful heart.

A grateful heart doesn't search for what's missing, but delights in what's present. A grateful heart expects the best from others, and gives its best in return. A grateful heart forgets what might have been, and enjoys every moment of each new day as it comes. A grateful heart is a prayer of its own—one that fills the heavens with praise!

Perhaps nothing robs us of our grateful attitude as quickly as comparing ourselves with others. The Bible reminds us again and again that we are not to covet what others have nor compare ourselves to them, but our human nature brings such thoughts to mind repeatedly. Through prayer, we can ask God to take away our desire for things we don't have, and He will. We will soon make a habit of being grateful before we grumble if we focus on all the things for which we are grateful instead of focusing on how much better we think things could be.

If we really work at it, we can even be grateful for all the aches and pains that accompany growing older! After all, growing old is not a right, it is a privilege not everyone is granted. If God has allowed us to grow old gracefully—perhaps even giving us an abundance of grandchildren and great-grandchildren—we are blessed beyond belief. That alone should help us to replace our grumbling about aging with an attitude of gratitude for the gift of a long and productive life.

For Reflection or Discussion

- In what ways can we express our gratitude to God?
- As you look back over your life, can you think of times when you were blessed by God, but took His blessings for granted?
- Is there anything in your life now for which you have forgotten to thank God? Let your thanksgiving praise Him now.

A Thought to Share

An attitude of gratitude can be contagious! Tell those who mean the most to you how grateful you are for them and then watch the gratitude spread.

Suggestion for the Week

Before going to bed each night this week, make a list of five things for which you are grateful. They can be small things or big things—anything counts!

Suggested Hymns

- For the Beauty of the Earth
- Come, Ye Thankful People, Come
- We Gather Together

Prayer Requests and Closing Prayer

LESSON 54
Celebrating a
Christ-Centered Christmas

KEY VERSE

"For God so loved the world that he gave his one and only Son, that whoever believes in him shall not perish but have eternal life."
JOHN 3:16

OPENING PRAYER

LORD, EVEN WHEN WE'VE SLOWED DOWN the pace of our lives, it's still possible for us to get caught up in all the hustle and bustle of Christmas and forget the true purpose of the season. Keep us close to You, Lord. Help us to focus on who You are, and on what You came to earth to do for us. In Your holy name we pray, amen.

INTRODUCTION

A popular slogan at this time of year among Christians is, "Jesus is the reason for the season." We see nativity sets on display and sing familiar Christmas carols. But do we really focus on Christ or is He just another character in the age-old Bethlehem story?

A woman who collected different types of nativity sets was dismayed one year that she couldn't find the Baby Jesus for one of the crèche scenes. After searching high and low she finally gave away the rest of the set—after all, what good was it without Jesus? The next year, when she was unwrapping her collection of nativity sets, she found the missing Baby Jesus tightly swaddled in a piece of bubble wrap she had overlooked before. Rather than be dismayed that the set was now gone, she decided everyone could use "a little extra Jesus" at Christmas time. The lonely neighbor next door? She could use a little extra Jesus. So could soldiers stationed far away from their families or children in foster care…the list is endless really. So she kept the small figure of Baby Jesus in the manger to remind her of that truth.

What about you? What reminders will you have this season to keep Jesus at the center of your Christmas celebration? How will you maintain a Christ-centered Christmas in the midst of the holiday happenings? We have to make a concerted effort to keep the world from taking Christ out of Christmas. While joyous and cheerful, all the distractions are just that—attempts to rob us of the true gift of peace that Christmas brings.

FOR REFLECTION OR DISCUSSION

- Why do you think it's so hard for us to stay focused on Christ during the Christmas season?
- Do you think keeping the focus on Christ was as difficult when you were rearing children as it is today?
- Did you have certain traditions in your home or church to keep Christ the center of Christmas?

SCRIPTURES AND QUOTES

For to us a child is born, to us a son is given, and the government will be on his shoulders. And he will be called Wonderful Counselor, Mighty God, Everlasting Father, Prince of Peace.
ISAIAH 9:6

"I bring you good news of great joy that will be for all the people. Today in the town of David a Savior has been born to you; he is Christ the Lord."
LUKE 2:10

In the beginning was the Word and the Word was with God and the Word was God. He was with God in the beginning. Through him all things were made; without him nothing was made that has been made.
JOHN 1:1-3

*The Word became flesh and made his dwelling among us. We have
seen his glory, the glory of the One and Only,
who came from the Father, full of grace and truth.*
JOHN 1:14

Jesus Christ is the same yesterday and today and forever.
HEBREWS 13:8

*"I am the Alpha and the Omega, the First and the Last,
the Beginning and the End."*
REVELATION 22:13

*Then let every heart keep Christmas within. Christ's pity for sorrow,
Christ's hatred for sin, Christ's care for the weakest, Christ's courage
for right. Everywhere, everywhere, Christmas tonight!*
PHILLIPS BROOKS

MEDITATION

If Jesus Christ isn't the focus of our lives the other days of the
year, He won't be our focus on Christmas either. We need to keep
the truth of who He is in our hearts and minds all year long. To stay
centered on Him, we need to accept that He was, and is, and is to be.
Once we do that, we can thank Him for the past, abide with Him in
the present, and trust Him with the future.

First, we thank Him for the past. Think back over all the
Christmas mornings you've experienced. Who has Jesus been to you
in Christmases past? Hopefully, most of your memories are happy
ones, but if you had some disappointing Christmases, Jesus was there,
too, and knows the pain you felt. Once we give our lives to Christ, He
can heal our hurts. Praise Him for being with you in the past.

Second, we have to acknowledge who He is in the present. Who
is He in your life today? We learn a lot about who Christ is when we
abide in Him. In John 15:5 KJV Jesus said, *"Abide in me, and I in
you. As the branch cannot bear fruit of itself, except it abide in the vine;
no more can ye, except ye abide in me."* We need to spend time with
the Lord if we are really to know who He is, and we must discipline
ourselves to keep our thoughts on Him. Through the Holy Spirit
dwelling within us, we feel His presence always—guiding us, directing

us, comforting us. As the old hymn says, "He walks with me, and He talks with me, and He tells me I am His own." That's knowing Christ in the present.

Lastly, we can take comfort in thinking about who Jesus Christ will be to us in the future. He promised that He was going to heaven to prepare a place for us (John 14:2)—and that He would come back to claim us as His own and make us co-heirs with Him of all the treasures of heaven (Romans 8:16-17). The basis of our hope for eternal life is in the promises of Jesus, and He can be trusted.

So thank Him for the past, abide with Him in the present, trust Him with the future, and you will have a very Christ-centered Christmas.

FOR REFLECTION OR DISCUSSION

- What one thing could you do to keep yourself focused on Christ this Christmas?
- Are you confident you will have eternal life with Jesus Christ? Why or why not? (If you haven't given your life to Him and accepted His gift of salvation, Christmas is a wonderful time to do that.)
- Is there some way for us to keep a bit of Christmas in our hearts all year long? Share your thoughts.

A THOUGHT TO SHARE

Christ is the heart of Christmas. Without Him, it isn't Christmas at all.

SUGGESTION FOR THE WEEK

As you go about the activities of Christmas week, simply ask the Lord to be present in your heart. You will not be disappointed!

SUGGESTED HYMNS

- O Come, All Ye Faithful
- Silent Night! Holy Night!
- The First Noel

PRAYER REQUESTS AND CLOSING PRAYER

LESSON 55
To Love and Be Loved

KEY VERSE

We love because he first loved us.
1 JOHN 4:19

OPENING PRAYER

O LORD, HOW GRATEFUL WE ARE for Your love for us. May we embrace Your love, and fill ourselves with it, that it might spill out of us into the lives of all those whom we encounter. We love You, Lord. In Your name we pray, amen.

INTRODUCTION

This time of year there is a lot of emphasis on love in our society, but too often the focus is on romantic love and little thought is given to the other types of love in the world. The loves of husband and wife, of parent and child, of grandparent and grandchild, and of one friend for another are all incredible forces of love worth celebrating.

As we age, we may have the most opportunity to show love to friends old and new. When friendship and love work together, it's as if we are wrapping a warm quilt of encouragement around others. Our actions are the squares in that quilt, and love is the thread that connects them.

You may not realize how often your acts of friendship have just enough of God's love in them to turn them into quilts of encouragement, but they do. The little things you do make the difference.

For example, out of friendship you may pick up the phone to call a friend who's depressed. Out of love, you stay on the phone longer than you intended because you sense your friend needs to talk.

So this Valentine's Day, when love is in the air, be open to all its many faces and enjoy loving others even as others love you! Remember that when all our memories of human love are collected like so many heart-shaped valentines in a shoe box, they can't begin to compare with the love our heavenly Father has for us. That's the most enduring love of all.

FOR REFLECTION OR DISCUSSION

- How do you notice the world distorting the meaning of love?
- Has your capacity to love others increased or diminished over the years? Why do you think this is true?
- How has your concept of love changed as you've aged?

SCRIPTURES AND QUOTES

"I have loved you with an everlasting love;
I have drawn you with loving-kindness."
JEREMIAH 31:3

"The Lord your God is with you, he is mighty to save.
He will take great delight in you, he will quiet you with his love,
he will rejoice over you with singing."
ZEPHANIAH 3:17

"For God so loved the world that he gave his one and only Son, that
whoever believes in him shall not perish but have eternal life."
JOHN 3:16

And now these three remain: faith, hope and love.
But the greatest of these is love.
I CORINTHIANS 13:13

The only thing that counts is faith expressing itself through love.
GALATIANS 5:6

Dear friends, let us love one another, for love comes from God. Everyone who loves has been born of God and knows God. Whoever does not love does not know God, because God is love.
1 JOHN 4:7-8

With all our hearts and souls, all our minds and all our strength, all our understanding, with every faculty and every effort, with every affection and all our emotions, with every wish and every desire, we should love our Lord and God who gives us everything, body and soul, and all our life; it was He who created and redeemed us and of His mercy alone He will save us.
ST. FRANCIS OF ASSISI

MEDITATION

Jesus was the perfect model of how we are to love, and He asked us to love ourselves, love others, and love God.

First, love ourselves. In Mark 12:31, Jesus said, *"Love your neighbor as yourself."* Yet because of messages we heard as a child, old wounds, failures, or even sin, we sometimes find it hard to love ourselves. That's when we need to remember that we can love ourselves because God first loved us. His love is unconditional. He loves us so much that He sent Jesus to die for us so that we could dwell in His presence for eternity. He loves us enough to convict us of our sins and free us from even the guilt of them. He loves us enough to indwell us with the Holy Spirit to comfort and guide us. He loves us enough to give us people to love and to be loved by, work to do, and a Creation to explore.

All the theologians in the world couldn't come up with a more profound statement about His love than the words of the children's song: "Jesus loves me, this I know, for the Bible tells me so." God loves us, and so we can love ourselves.

Second, we are to love others. In John 13:34, Jesus said, *"A new command I give you: Love one another."* Some people are easier to love than others are, but we are even to love the unlovable. It may not be realistic to believe that we will be able to love everyone we encounter unconditionally, but it is realistic to believe that we can consider choosing love as our first response in every situation. What a difference that would make in our daily lives!

Finally, we are to love God. In Matthew 22:37, Jesus said, *"Love the Lord your God with all your heart and with all your soul and with all your mind."* He called this the first and greatest commandment. We love God when we worship Him and give Him praise. We love Him when we obey Him and trust Him with our past, our present, and our future. That kind of love lasts. It's a love worth celebrating today and every day.

For Reflection or Discussion

- God finds each of us lovable. Why, then, do we sometimes find it so hard to love ourselves? What gets in the way?
- Think of a difficult situation or confrontation in which you found yourself this past week. How would it have turned out differently if love had been your first response?
- What kinds of things keep us from "loving the unlovable?" How do you demonstrate your love for God?

A Thought to Share

Jesus loves me, this I know. Jesus knows me, this I love.

Suggestion for the Week

How can you show the love of God to someone this week? Open your heart, mind and soul to all the possible ways to love someone as God loves them.

Suggested Hymns

- Love Divine, All Loves Excelling
- Love Lifted Me
- O, How I Love Jesus

Prayer Requests and Closing Prayer

LESSON 56
Easter Joy!

KEY VERSE

*This is how God showed his love among us: He sent his one and only
Son into the world that we might live through him.*
1 JOHN 4:9

OPENING PRAYER

O LORD, AS WE ENTER into this blessed Easter season, we reflect
anew on the marvelous gift You brought to our world—the gift
of eternal salvation through Your Son, Jesus Christ. Keep us ever
mindful of the many blessings that are ours, Lord. Fill us with joy
as we celebrate the Good News of Easter. In Your precious name we
pray, amen.

INTRODUCTION

A good part of this world would have us celebrating bunnies
and baby chicks, jellybeans and colorfully decorated eggs this Easter
season. However, those who believe in Jesus Christ and know of His
love for them have so much more to celebrate! Certainly, there is
nothing wrong with bunnies, chicks and eggs—after all, they are all a
part of God's amazing Creation and He wants us to delight in them.
Yet we are missing the greatest gift ever given if that's all Easter means
to us.

Some may reject the Good News of Easter because it seems far
too simple, or too good to be true. They can't accept that they don't
have to earn their way into God's good graces, or jump through
certain hoops to get into heaven. The cynicism of our culture obscures

the truth that they are being offered a free gift, and all they have to do is accept it.

When God allowed sin to enter the world He created, He knew He would have to find a way to bridge the gap sin placed between Him and the men and women He also created and loved. He sent Jesus into the world to bridge that gap for us—to die on the cross to bear all our sins so that we can enter into God's presence sinless and forgiven. The Bible is full of confirmation that God knew His plan for our salvation from the beginning, and that Jesus Christ is truly the Alpha, the beginning, and the Omega, the end.

If you have lived your life without accepting the gift of salvation God is offering to you, what better time to accept it than at Easter? Simply ask Jesus Christ to be Lord of your life. Ask Him to forgive you for all your sins, and to accept you into His eternal glory. If you do, this will be the best Easter you will ever celebrate for you will be celebrating it along with the whole family of God.

For Reflection or Discussion

- Many families have special traditions around the celebration of Easter. What traditions did you celebrate as a child or with your family as an adult?
- What do you think prevents people from accepting the Good News of Easter?
- Is Easter just one day out of the year, or is there such a thing as "everyday Easter?"

Scriptures and Quotes

But he was pierced for our transgressions, he was crushed for our iniquities; the punishment that brought us peace was upon him, and by his wounds we are healed.
ISAIAH 53:5

"Behold the Lamb of God, which taketh away the sin of the world."
JOHN 1:29 (KJV)

"For God so loved the world that he gave his one and only Son, that whoever believes in him shall not perish but have eternal life."
JOHN 3:16

"Now this is eternal life: that they may know you, the only true God, and Jesus Christ, whom you have sent."
JOHN 17:3

But God demonstrates his own love for us in this:
While we were still sinners, Christ died for us.
ROMANS 5:8

Just as Christ was raised from the dead through the glory of the Father, we too may live a new life.
ROMANS 6:4

We are to, and may, live nobly now because we are to live forever.
PHILLIPS BROOKS

The story of Easter is the story of God's wonderful window of divine surprise! [76]
CARL KNUDSEN

Our Lord has written the promise of the Resurrection, not in books alone, but in every leaf in springtime.
MARTIN LUTHER

We are an Easter people, and alleluia is our song!
ST. AUGUSTINE

MEDITATION

How astounding it is that the Good News of Easter is not just to bring us comfort when someone we love dies, or when we ourselves are preparing to pass over into eternity in heaven. The Good News of Easter is that once we believe in Jesus Christ we are *already* living an eternal life—right here on earth.

If we really grasped this truth, wouldn't it completely transform the way we live out each and every day? When a friend disappointed us when we needed her most, we'd be able to forgive her much more quickly with an eternal perspective. When we felt our bones creaking as we got out of bed, we'd think of those creaks as the normal shortcomings of temporary housing—not part of our eternal state of being.

There is a touching account of a family learning to live without the daily presence of their husband and father who died while serving with the U.S. Army in Iraq. The soldier's four-year-old son repeatedly heard, over the period of a few days, that his dad was now in heaven. Finally, he asked the only logical question: "Then why don't we just go there and pick him up?"

Unfortunately, it's not easy to span the distance between our earthly existence and our eternal home. But we can find great comfort in accepting the truth that we live one life in Christ—whether here or there, we are alive because He died on the cross for us, and rose again from the dead on Easter morning.

Paul wrote in Romans 5:1-2: *Therefore, since we have been justified through faith, we have peace with God through our Lord Jesus Christ, through whom we have gained access by faith into this grace in which we now stand.*

What comfort in knowing we are NOW standing in God's grace, right in the middle of His will for our lives.

On Easter Sunday when we sing our favorite hymns and glory in the truth of the Good News of Easter, may we also pledge anew to live every day of the coming year as people who are already dwelling in eternal glory. The Good News of Easter speaks to our hearts as nothing else can. Rejoice!

FOR REFLECTION OR DISCUSSION

- If we agree with St. Augustine that "we are an Easter people," how should that reality change the way we live each day?
- Some people believe the Good News is for others, but not for them. How can we be sure that Christ died for *all* our sins, past, present and future?

- What one part of the Easter message will you cling to most closely this year?

A Thought to Share

Easter is a promise kept.

Suggestion for the Week

Look for an opportunity to share the Good News of Easter with someone you encounter this week. Remember to tell them they can begin living an eternal life right now—not just when they die!

Suggested Hymns

- Christ the Lord Is Risen Today
- He Lives
- Crown Him with Many Crowns

Prayer Requests and Closing Prayer

NOTES

LESSON 57
Freedom in the Lord

KEY VERSE

"So if the Son sets you free, you will be free indeed."
JOHN 8:36

OPENING PRAYER

O LORD, THE WORLD IN WHICH WE LIVE strives to keep us in bondage to many different sins and desires. But we know that because of Your sacrifice for us, we are free! Thank You, Lord, for allowing us to walk in Your freedom. In Your precious name we pray, amen.

INTRODUCTION

We are so blessed to live in a country where we are free to assemble, free to pray, free to follow the religion of our choice, and free to express ourselves to others. In fact, the freedoms we enjoy here are too numerous to list, and are often only appreciated when contrasted with the lack of freedom in other countries and societies. All we have to do is hear the evening news or pick up a newspaper to realize that not everyone in the world enjoys the same freedom that we have—and can too easily come to take for granted.

On Memorial Day, the Fourth of July, or Veterans Day, we pause to remember those in our history who played a part in securing our freedom. The founders of our country were, for the most part, God-fearing men who prayed before every action they took. George Washington wrote, "It is the duty of all nations to acknowledge the providence of Almighty God, to obey His will, to be grateful for His benefits, and humbly to implore His protection and favor."

The soldiers who served and died in WWI, WWII, Vietnam, Korea, Iraq and Afghanistan, as well as in other conflicts, know all too well the price of freedom, and that freedom isn't free.

It's said that, for those who risked their lives to preserve our freedom, it has a special meaning that those of us who never served, but only reap the benefits of their service, will never know.

But those who believe in Jesus Christ as Lord and Savior know a freedom that surpasses all the political and religious freedom we enjoy here on earth. They know the freedom from sin.

For Reflection or Discussion

- Did you or anyone in your family ever serve in the armed forces? If so, when and where?
- What sacrifices did you or they make in service to our country?
- Why do you think Americans often take our freedoms for granted?

Scriptures and Quotes

I run in the path of your commands, for you have set my heart free.
Psalm 119:32

I will walk about in freedom, for I have sought out your precepts.
Psalm 119:45

"If you hold to my teaching, you are really my disciples.
Then you will know the truth, and the truth will set you free."
John 8:31-32

You have been set free from sin and have become slaves to righteousness.
Romans 6:18

Now the Lord is the Spirit, and where the
Spirit of the Lord is, there is freedom.
2 Corinthians 3:17

It is for freedom that Christ has set us free.
GALATIANS 5:1

*To him who loves us and has freed us from our sins by his blood,
and has made us to be a kingdom and priests to serve his God and
Father—to him be glory and power for ever and ever! Amen.*
REVELATION 1:5-6

*If we are free with the liberty of Christ, others will be brought
into that same liberty—the liberty of realizing
the dominance of Jesus Christ.* [77]
OSWALD CHAMBERS

MEDITATION

For followers of Jesus Christ, the word freedom has a meaning
that far surpasses the freedom we have as citizens of a free nation.
Those who have accepted His invitation to follow Him know so many
freedoms we can barely imagine them all.

We have freedom from sin, because we have the Holy Spirit
to convict us of sinful behaviors and lead us away from them. We
have freedom from our past mistakes because we have the complete
forgiveness of God through the intervention of Jesus—who promises
to present us before the Father's throne as spotless and pure. We have
freedom from fear because we know that we are never alone. The Lord
is always with us, and His will shall be done. We have freedom from
the bondage of addiction, abuse, and any number of other harmful
conditions, because we have the power of the living Lord to overcome
any bondage Satan can throw at us.

Most glorious of all, we have freedom from death, because we
know that those who believe in Jesus Christ will join Him in heaven
and have eternal life. That's a freedom worth celebrating, is it not?

We know we have these freedoms, but are we really living as free
people who answer only to God? Do we walk daily with the Lord who
sacrificed all so that we might be free? Our task is to live as people
who are truly free, as difficult as it may be at times. To embrace the
freedom we have and share it with all those with whom we come in

contact. Freedom is a gift. Freedom in the Lord is the greatest gift of all.

For Reflection or Discussion

- Why do you think we sometimes feel like we are in bondage? What things tend to bind you?
- How can we begin to live as beloved, free children of God?
- What freedom that you have in Christ means the most to you, and why?

A Thought to Share

Freedom is never free. Christ paid the price for ours.

Suggestion for the Week

As you are visiting with those you know, be alert to whatever is binding them, and remind them gently that they can be free in Christ!

Suggested Hymns

- Battle Hymn of the Republic
- God Bless America
- My Country, 'Tis of Thee

Prayer Requests and Closing Prayer

About the Author

Nancy Parker Brummett first led a Bible study in an assisted living setting in 1999 and she and the Lord developed *The Hope of Glory* in the years following. She gained a heart for older adults as a child because her grandmother lived with her family, and she has enjoyed close friendships with many older adults over the years. She also journeyed with her mother and mother-in-law through their adventures in aging. Her academic interest in aging led her to receive the Professional Advancement Certificate in Gerontology from the University of Colorado at Colorado Springs.

An author and freelance writer living in Colorado Springs, CO, Nancy's other books include *Simply the Savior*, *It Takes a Home*, *The Journey of Elisa* and *Reconcilable Differences*. She is now focusing her writing and speaking ministries on her passion for older adults and those who care for them. She and her husband Jim have four grown children, 12 grandchildren, and two cats in their blended family. To learn more about Nancy's life and work or to subscribe to her blog on aging issues, "Take My Hand Again," visit her website at:

www.nancyparkerbrummett.com.

Endnotes

1. Robert Durback, Editor, *Seeds of Hope: A Henri Nouwen Reader*, (New York: Doubleday, 1997), 188.

2. L.B. Cowman, *Streams in the Desert*, (Grand Rapids, Michigan: Zondervan Publishing House, 1997), 227.

3. Frank S. Mead, *12,000 Religious Quotations*, (Grand Rapids, Michigan: Baker Books, 1989), 345.

4. Watchman Nee, *The Normal Christian Life*, (Carol Stream, Illinois: Tyndale House Publishers, 1977), 217.

5. Andrew Murray, *Abide in Christ*, (Springdale, Pennsylvania: Whitaker House, 1979), 169.

6. Dietrich Bonhoeffer, *Life Together*, (New York: Harper & Row, 1954), 21.

7. Hannah Whitall Smith, *The Christian's Secret of a Happy Life*, (Grand Rapids, Michigan: Fleming H. Revell, 1952), 15.

8. Chuck Colson, www.breakpoint.org, October 11, 2006.

9. Nee, *The Normal Christian Life*, 104.

10. Harry Verploegh, Editor, *Oswald Chambers: The Best from All His Books*, (Nashville, Tennessee: Thomas Nelson Publishers, 1987), 172.

11. "Sisters," (Minnesota: Heartland Samplers, Inc., 1995), May 5.

12. Oswald Chambers, *My Utmost for His Highest*, (Westwood, New Jersey: Barbour and Company, Inc., 1963), 242.

13. Henry T. Blackaby and Claude V. King, *Experiencing God*, (Nashville, Tennessee: LifeWay, 1990), 45.

14. J. I. Packer, *Knowing God*, (Downers Grove, Illinois; InterVarsity Press, 1973), 29.

15. Ibid, 37.

16.   *Today's Dictionary of the Bible*, (Minneapolis, Minnesota: Bethany House Publishers, 1982), 189.

17.   Walter A. Henrichsen, *Thoughts from the Diary of a Desperate Man*, (El Cajon, California: Leadership Foundation, 2006), 39.

18.   Chambers, *My Utmost for His Highest*, 229.

19.   Cowman, *Streams in the Desert*, 462.

20.   Mother Teresa, www.goodreads.com/quotes/show/18064.

21.   Mead, *12,000 Religious Quotations*, 450.

22.   Chambers, *My Utmost for His Highest*, 225.

23.   Smith, *The Christian's Secret of a Happy Life*, 221.

24.   Mead, *12,000 Religious Quotations*, 259.

25.   Angela Thomas, *Choosing Joy: A 52-Week Devotional for Discovering True Happiness, Book 2*, (New York: Howard Books, 2011), 208.

26.   Blackaby and King, *Experiencing God*, 83.

27.   Chambers, *My Utmost for His Highest*, 14.

28.   Mead, *12,000 Religious Quotations*, 189.

29.   Joni Eareckson Tada, *Heaven Your Real Home*, (Grand Rapids, Michigan: Zondervan, 2001), 34.

30.   Ibid., 35.

31.   Ibid., 209-210.

32.   Chambers, *My Utmost for His Highest*, 215.

33.   Blaise Pascal, *Pensées*, 10.148.

34.   G.K. Chesterton paraphrase, (Christiantimelines.com, "Searching for God," 2008).

35.   Chambers, *My Utmost for His Highest*, 234.

36.   Bruce Main, *Spotting the Sacred*, (Grand Rapids, Michigan: Baker Books, 2006), 17.

37.   Ibid., 19.

38.   Ibid., 246.

39.   Henri M. Nouwen and Walter J. Gaffney, *Aging*, (New York: Doubleday, 1974), 17.

40.   Eleanor Roosevelt, http://www.goodreads.com/quotes/show/20391.

41.   Gary Smalley and John Trent, Phd., *The Gift of the Blessing*, (Nashville, Tennessee: Thomas Nelson Publishers, 1993).

42.   Chambers, *My Utmost for His Highest*, 78.

43.   Ibid., 244.

44.   Richard J. Foster, *Freedom of Simplicity*, (New York: Harper & Row, 1981), 143.

45.   Chambers, *My Utmost for His Highest*, 357.

46.   Point of Grace, "Heal the Wound," 2007 Word Music.

47.   Mead, *12,000 Religious Quotations*, 213.

48.   Chambers, *My Utmost for His Highest*, 306.

49.   Lloyd John Ogilvie, *Autobiography of God*, (Ventura, California: Regal Books, 1979), 301.

50.   Charles F. Stanley, www.inspiration-for-singles.com/self-confidence.html.

51.   Nee, *The Normal Christian Life*, 176-177.

52.   Steven Curtis Chapman, www.stevencurtischapman.com.

53.   Elisabeth Kübler-Ross, *On Death and Dying*, (New York, New York: McMillan Publishing Co., Inc., 1969).

54.   Chambers, *My Utmost for His Highest*, 366.

55.   Blackaby and King, *Experiencing God*, 86.

56.   Charles R. Swindoll, "Creating a Legacy: Preparing the Stones," *Insights*, January 2004.

57.   Ibid.

58.   Swindoll, http://www.mentoring-disciples.org/Quotes.html.

59.   Arthur W. Pink, http://transfigurations.blogspot.
      com/2010/05/devotional-before-he-furnishes-abundant.html

60.   Chambers, *My Utmost for His Highest*, 7.

61.   Ibid., 97.

62.   Eugene Peterson, *A Long Obedience in the Same Direction*,
      (Downers Grove, Illinois: InterVarsity Press, 2000), 90.

63.   Cowman, *Streams in the Desert*, 406.

64.   Murray, *Abide in Christ*, 54.

65.   Mead, *12,000 Religious Quotations*, 183.

66.   *The Hymnal for Worship & Celebration*, (Nashville, Tennessee:
      Word Music, 1986), 539.

67.   Ibid., 337.

68.   Ibid., 497.

69.   Ibid., 503.

70.   Murray, *Abide in Christ*, 24.

71.   Ibid., 33.

72.   Ibid., 5.

73.   Mead, *12,000 Religious Quotations*, 204.

74.   Kelly Hall, *Courageous Faith*, (Colorado Springs, Colorado:
      Dawson Media, 2010), 103.

75.   Ruth Myers, *31 Days of Praise*, (Sisters, Oregon: Multnomah
      Books, 1994), 150.

76.   Mead, *12,000 Religious Quotations*, 120.

77.   Chambers, *My Utmost for His Highest*, 127.

44657272R00165

Made in the USA
San Bernardino, CA
19 January 2017